AS THE ROMANS DO

La Dolce Vita in a Cookbook
Classic and Reinvented Recipes from Rome

ELEONORA GALASSO

Photography by David Loftus

To .... stars

....

First published in Great Britain in 2016 by
Mitchell Beazley, a division of Octopus Publishing Group Ltd
Carmelite House
50 Victoria Embankment
London EC4Y 0DZ
www.octopusbooks.co.uk

ISBN 978 1 78472 138 1

A CIP catalogue record for this book is available from
the British Library.

Printed and bound in China

10 9 8 7 6 5 4 3 2 1

Senior Commissioning Editor: Eleanor Maxfield
Art Director: Juliette Norsworthy
Senior Editor: Alex Stetter
Copy Editor: Simon Davis
Photographer: David Loftus (except pp 8, 11, 65 top right and
153 bottom left: Cecilia Fusco; p 302 top row centre: Olivia Magris)
Home Economists and Food Stylists: Emily Ezekiel, Sian Henley
Props Stylist: Linda Berlin
Illustrator: Grace Helmer
Assistant Production Manager: Caroline Alberti

AS THE ROMANS DO

La Dolce Vita in a Cookbook
Classic and Reinvented Recipes from Rome

ELEONORA GALASSO

Photography by David Loftus

MITCHELL BEAZLEY

CONTENTS

Introduction.................................8
The Roman cupboard..................12

CHAPTER 1
BREAKFAST RITUAL
AL BAR.............................. 14

Maritozzi 18
Sticky buns

Ventagli 20
Flaky pastry fans

Granola 22
Granola

**Treccia di brioche con scaglie
di cioccolato** 25
Brioche braid with chocolate flakes

Biscotti brutti ma buoni 26
Ugly but good biscuits

Bignè di San Giuseppe 30
St Joseph's Day cream puffs

Bomboloni 31
Baked doughnuts

Biscottoni da inzuppo 32
Dunking biscuits

Fette biscottate 35
Sweet melba toast

Budini di riso.........................36
Rice pudding tartlets

CHAPTER 2
MERENDE 38

Tarallucci al vino 43
Baked sweet wine pretzels

**Insalata di farro con pollo, zucchine
e formaggio di capra** 44
Spelt salad with chicken, courgettes
& goats' cheese

Trio di bruschette 46
Three bruschette of a kind

**Torta rustica carciofi, piselli
e prosciutto**............................50
Savoury pie with artichokes, peas
& ham

Tortino di verdure incartato 51
Wrapped vegetable pie

Pizzette rosse..........................55
Mini pizzas with tomato sauce

**Girelle di pan carrè con mousse di
prosciutto cotto agrumata** 56
Sandwich wheels with prosciutto mousse

Trio di ovis molis alle marmellate 57
Shortbread biscuit trio with jam

**Ciambellone di polenta alla zucca
e mele** 59
Polenta cake with pumpkin & apple

La pastiera 60
Wheat & candied fruit cake

CHAPTER 3
LUNCH ON THE RUN 62

Pomodori ripieni con patate 66
Rice-stuffed tomatoes with potatoes

**Rosetta con mortazza, stracchino
e mostarda casalinga** 69
Rosetta loaf with mortadella, stracchino
cheese & homemade mostarda

'Panino' di mozzarella......................... 71
Mozzarella 'sandwich'

**Conchiglioni ripieni su foglie
di basilico**................................72
Stuffed conchiglioni pasta on
basil leaves

Fagottini di verza ripieni 74
Savoy cabbage veal bundles

**Carpaccio di spigola con pesche,
kiwi e rughetta** 75
Sea bass carpaccio with peaches, kiwi
& rocket

Frittata di spaghetti............................79
Spaghetti omelette

**Soppressata di polpo con insalata di
patate e sedano** 80
Octopus 'kebab' with potato
& celery salad

Melanzane e zucchine a barchetta 84
Aubergine & courgette 'boats'

Gnocchi alla ricotta del giovedì con gamberetti e pistacchi...........................86
Thursday's ricotta gnocchi with prawns & pistachios

Ceci e baccalà.....................................89
Friday's salt cod with chickpeas

CHAPTER 4
FAMILY LUNCHES..............90

Gnocchi alla Romana con sugo di spuntature di maiale..........................94
Roman-style semolina gnocchi with pork rib sauce

Coda di rospo agli agrumi e finocchio accompagnata da fagiolini corallo in salsa di noci, melograno e mango........96
Citrusy monkfish with fennel accompanied by runner beans in a walnut, mango & pomegranate dressing

Spiedini di manzo ripieni con tortino di agretti......................................98
Filled beef rolls with agretti tart

Pasta al forno con asparagi, pancetta e provola.........................103
Baked pasta with asparagus, pancetta & provola cheese

Filetto di salmone con mousse di fave e pecorino.............................104
Salmon fillet with broad bean & pecorino mousse

Pasta alla carbonara.........................106
Pasta with carbonara sauce

Spezzatino in umido con parmigiana di carciofi........................108
Beef stew with artichoke parmigiana

Pesce spada al cartoccio con polpo e scarola in padella..............................112
Swordfish en papillote with octopus & sautéed lettuce

Pasticcio di cappelletti panna, prosciutto, fegatini e piselli................114
Cappelletti pasta cake with cream, ham, liver & peas

Polpette della Nonna accompagnate da scalogni glassati con prugne secche................................117
Grandma's meatballs with glazed shallots & prunes

Vitel tonné...118
Tuna-sauced veal

Insalata di puntarelle........................120
Puntarelle salad

Cannelloni al forno con ricotta e zafferano..121
Ricotta & saffron cannelloni

Coda alla vaccinara in verde............124
Green oxtail stew

Biancomangiare................................125
White soup

CHAPTER 5
APERITIVO......................126

Mozzarella in carrozza......................131
Mozzarella in a carriage

Panzanella..132
Bread salad

Trio di fritti: Supplì al telefono, crocchette di patate e schiacciatine di bollito...................134
Fritter trio of Roman-style rice balls, potato croquettes & mini meat loaves

Olive all'ascolana...............................137
Ascoli-style stuffed olives

Fiori di zucca ripieni..........................139
Stuffed courgette flowers

Galantina di pollo servita con bocconcini d'uva al formaggio..........142
Chicken galantine with cheesy grapes

Sandwich di polenta con salsiccia e formaggio...145
Polenta sandwich with baked sausage & cheese

Tramezzini...146
Tea sandwiches

Alici o sardine marinate...................147
Marinated anchovies or sardines

Limoni ripieni alla crema di tonno..149
Lemons filled with tuna cream

CHAPTER 6
ROMANTIC DINNERS ..150

**Bucatini alle vongole e patate
alla menta** 154
Bucatini with clams & minty potatoes

Ossobuco al pepe verde e vignarola ...157
Roman-style ossobuco with vignarola

**Pasta e ceci, salvia e fagioli del
purgatorio con tartufo nero e lardo** ... 158
Pasta, chickpeas & beans with black
truffles & lardo

Orata in crosta di patate 161
Seabream in a potato crust

**Costolette d'agnello in crosta con
cavolfiore e castagne accompagnate
da gattò di patate, cardi e arance** 164
Crispy lamb cutlets with cauliflower
& chestnuts accompanied by a potato
& orange savoury cake

**Ravioli alla Romana con broccoli,
alici, pomodori secchi e ricotta**........ 168
Roman-style ravioli with broccoli,
anchovies, sun-dried tomatoes & ricotta

**Spiedini di anguille in foglie di
alloro e salsa al cren** 170
Eel & bay leaf skewers with
homemade horseradish sauce

Penne gratinate alla Campolattaro ...171
Campolattaro-style penne gratin

**Seppioline piselli, avocado
e pomodoro**.......................... 173
Squid with peas, avocado & tomatoes

CHAPTER 7
**#FOODHAPPINESS
SUPPERS** 174

Pollo alla Romana con peperoni 179
Roman-style chicken with peppers

Pasta cacio, pepe e cozze....................181
Pasta with cheese, pepper & mussels

**Braciole di maiale con
panuntelle**.......................... 183
Pork chops with greased bread

**Tesoro di riso e sogliole con salsa
al prosecco** 184
Rice & lemon sole timbale with
prosecco gravy

**Porchetta di Ariccia e cavoli
trascinati** 188
Ariccia-style roast pork with
'dragged' Savoy cabbage

**Maccheroni alla Gricia con carciofi,
zucchine e ricotta salata** 192
Maccheroni with artichokes,
courgettes & ricotta salata

Pasta all'Amatriciana 193
Pasta with Amatriciana sauce

**Coniglio brodettato della
vendemmia con uva e olive** 194
Stewed rabbit with grapes & olives

Ribollita Laziale 196
Lazio-style Ribollita soup

CHAPTER 8
FESTIVITIES 198

Palline ricotta e cocco 202
Ricotta & coconut balls

**Mimosa al profumo di ananas
con fiorellini zuccherati** 204
Pineapple-flavoured mimosa cake
with candied flowers

Cuzzupa Pasquale 207
Easter bread with eggs

**Pane di Pasqua con pecorino,
miele e salame** 211
Easter bread with pecorino cheese,
honey & salami

**Lumaca di pangiallo Romanesco
dell'imperatore con gelatina
di mandarini**.. 212
Imperial-style sweet golden bread
with clementine jelly

Pesche sciroppate con panna 217
Poached peaches in syrup with cream

**Cotechino in crosta con insalata di
finocchi, olive, arance e melograno** ...218
Crusted cotechino with fennel, olive,
orange & pomegranate salad

Pesce finto di Natale 222
Christmas 'fish'

**Castagnole di carnevale alla
Romana** 223
Roman-style Carnival sweet dough balls

CHAPTER 9
CAKES & CO. 224

Fruttini gelato 229
Ice cream fruits

**Meringona alla Romana con salsa
di arance** 230
Roman-style meringue with
orange sauce

**Torta al cioccolato, amaretti
e tutti frutti** 233
Chocolate, amaretti
& tutti frutti cake

**Semifreddo ai cantucci
e Vin Santo** 237
Almond biscuit & sweet wine
semifreddo

Torta della nonna 238
Grandma's custard pie

**Crostata ricotta e cioccolato
come al ghetto** 240
Ghetto-style ricotta & chocolate pie

Tiramisù al Limone 241
Lemon tiramisù

**Torta di castagne e mele con farina
alle nocciole e arance candite** 244
Apple, chestnut & hazelnut cake
with candied oranges

Castagnaccio 245
Chestnut flour cake

Rotolo ricotta e visciole 247
Sour cherry & ricotta roll cake

CHAPTER 10
PROVISIONS 248

Carciofini sott'olio 252
Artichokes in oil

**Sugo passepartout per conserve,
pizza e pasta** 254
Passepartout tomato sauce
for preserves, pizza & pasta

**Tozzetti della Tuscia con
semi di chia** 257
Tuscan tozzetti biscuits
with chia seeds

Grissini 258
Breadsticks

Pangrattato 262
Breadcrumbs

Pesto Romano di zucchine 262
Roman-style courgette pesto

Crostini 263
Croutons

Conserva alla cipolla rossa 263
Red onion preserve

Marmellata di uva e noci pecan 265
Grape & pecan jam

Cubetti di ghiaccio 266
Handmade ice cubes

Il Negroni 268
Negroni cocktail

Sambuca alla Romana 271
Roman-style sambuca

CHAPTER 11
MIDNIGHT MUNCHIES..272

Grattachecca 276
Roman granita

Pallotte cacio e ova 278
Shallow-fried cheese & egg balls

**Straccetti al Marsala accompagnati
da spinaci e pane raffermo** 279
Sliced veal with Marsala accompanied
by spinach & stale bread

Carciofi alla Romana 283
Roman-style braised artichokes

**Salsiccia con lenticchie, porro
e finocchio** 284
Braised sausages with lentils, leeks
& fennel

Saltimbocca alla Romana 287
Roman-style saltimbocca

Pappa al pomodoro 288
Bread & tomato soup

**Fusilli lunghi aglio, olio, indivia,
peperoncino, capperi e molliche** 290
Fusilli pasta with garlic, olive oil,
endive, chillies, capers & breadcrumbs

Affogato al caffè 293
Ice-cream drowned in coffee

Sgroppino 295
Frothy lemon sorbet

Index 298
Acknowledgements................................... 303

INTRODUCTION

Food is a language and just like any other language, it needs to be decoded. I'm a Food Interpreter. Follow me and you will discover the secrets of the Roman table in all its wonderfully complex simplicity.

This book is for anyone who has ever wanted to make Italian food but was unsure where to start; it is also for anyone who thinks that Italian food is mostly about the joys of pasta and pizza. This book is for those unafraid to enter a new, hidden dimension of Italian gastronomic delights, from treats for early risers to dishes for midnight feasts, as well as revamped versions of classic recipes. My food is full of flavour and perfect for all home kitchens around the world. The recipes reflect authentic Italian home cooking, which requires no special ingredients or unusual equipment. Some recipes I inherited from my family, passed down from generation to generation, others I collected travelling around the Lazio region, accumulating secrets and techniques from an eclectic cast of characters for whom eating 'the Italian way' is not a lifestyle statement but a necessity.

The style of casual entertaining that can be found in households all over the world is simply magnified in Italy. I believe this is the reason behind the international love for Italian cuisine: it brings togetherness to a natural peak. Quality time spent with friends and family when time and space disappear to give way to good conversation, with everyone cooking together in the hustle and bustle of a kitchen that, no matter how big or how small, is always the heart of a home. Finally the words '*È pronto a tavola!*' are uttered, and when the meal is over there's a gratifying sense of contentment and of time well spent.

I divide my time between Rome, Paris and London, yet – much as I love travelling – there's not a corner on earth where I've seen the entire world pass by more than sitting at my own table. To me, it's a place from which to put the world to rights through sweet chats, sparkly exchanges or feisty debates that offers, above all, an uncontaminated, deep sense of participation. Each person is entitled to their own vision and each course has a story to tell: food is the key to unlocking life. My idea of the perfect meal is about achieving that sense of unconditional belonging, the search for which lets us all wander from land to land and, once that sense of 'home' is finally found, allows us to sit down and say: 'Hey, I quite like it here. I think I'm going to stay for a while.'

My recipes are down-to-earth and speak to the heart; easy on the wallet, unfussy meals for singles, couples, friends and families. You can play with the methods and adapt them to a variety of circumstances: quick and earthy breakfasts, vivacious *al fresco* meals, brilliant off-the-cuff dinner parties. It's all about finding your own food happiness, even if it's just an espresso and a spoonful of ricotta and honey – enjoy it with a grin on your face and a feeling of kitchen satisfaction as life takes on a different pace.

Rome is a layered city, the result of centuries of splendid and impressive urban chaos. It is bruised and magnified by all its eras, each of which has left its mark and an artful array of enveloping buildings and stirring personalities. There is classical Rome, the medieval city, the Renaissance, the Baroque, the Rome after 1870, when the city became the capital of the Kingdom of Italy. Then there is the Rome of *La Dolce Vita* – the cafés, the indomitably cheerful characters, the Vespas, the whistling at girls, the long walks in open-air museums and that inexplicable and enchanting confusion that takes possession of every visitor, leaving them spellbound.

I like to call myself a crusader of good food and eating well. *As The Romans Do* pays tribute to the mysteries behind the gastronomic culture of Rome and its surroundings – you'll feel like you're walking with me through the Roman breeze. I'll take you on a journey through the tiny side streets, the grand palazzos, the traditions, the communities and the hidden gems of this eternal city to discover what 'Romanity' is truly about. In Rome, the aroma of a strong coffee will wake me up, the fragrance of thin, oily *pizza bianca* will guide me through the morning and an indescribable mixture of burnt wood and tomato sauce will remind me that it's time for lunch. You don't need a watch in a city where time is marked by the smells drifting from kitchens and the ringing of church bells. When exploring the Roman way of life, keep your eyes, nose and ears wide open.

With this book, I set out to share atmospheres and fragrances that are familiar to me and that I hope will become just as familiar to you as you flip through the pages of this account of sweet idleness, or *dolce far niente*, as we say in Italy. Here is my quintessential *captatio benevolentiæ*: Cook, Eat and Talk. The Roman Way.

THE ROMAN CUPBOARD

There are some staples you will find in every Roman kitchen. Having the following items to hand will help you cook The Roman Way – these ingredients are the *sine qua non* for Roman epicurean living and becoming a food gladiator:

• When Romans say olive oil, we mean 'extra virgin cold-pressed olive oil'. The oil is extracted by pressing the olives without adding heat, thereby retaining their full nutritional value and aroma. Any dish will gain an unmistakable kick from this luminous golden condiment.

• Romans always keep at hand a cooking wine or *vino da cucina*, that is a cheap, full-flavoured wine from the local countryside. Not only is a good red wine stain on the tablecloth synonymous with a happy meal, we also use wine in many recipes, from stews to savoury pies.

• It goes without saying that eggs should be free-range if possible, but it's fundamental they are extra fresh and at room temperature.

• Romans love herbs – their perfume is so intoxicating – but we are not prescriptive about their use. You can't go wrong by adding basil, parsley, rosemary, thyme, sage or any fresh herb, you name it, to most dishes.

• Pasta is a fundamental component of any Italian pantry. We're not snobs about shapes and brands, but for special occasions, we'll treat ourselves. Pricier pasta is likely to have been made using the bronze wire-drawing method, which makes its surface rougher and allows it to hold sauces well. And once you've learned how to make your own pasta, you'll be able to produce as many variations on the theme as you wish.

• Use either carnaroli or arborio rice to ensure impeccable results for dishes from *timballi* to fried *supplì* (*see* pages 184 and 134).

• All Romans have a natural affinity for anchovies, perhaps because they featured as the main ingredient in *garum*, a sun-dried fermented fish sauce in vogue in Ancient Rome. Anchovies are perfect in salads, or as part of a luscious filling for fresh egg pasta.

• In many Roman households, a big batch of stock is prepared ahead of the coming culinary week. To make vegetable stock, half-fill a large saucepan with water, chuck in a peeled carrot, a celery stick, a tomato, a potato and a large peeled white onion studded with a few cloves, and cook everything for 20 minutes. It's that simple.

• *Soffritto* is a translucent combination of very finely chopped carrot, garlic, onion and celery that, added to a pan with some olive oil and allowed to sweat down for a few minutes, will transform the base of every sauce and condiment, whether vegetable-, fish- or meat-based.

• Ricotta (especially the kind made from sheep's milk) is something you buy as regularly in Rome as bread and onions. Use it to top your salads or add it to your pasta. Its flavour is so mild it gets on well with everything, from meat and fish dishes to cake or your breakfast toast.

• Romans keep jars and jars of tomato sauce in the pantry, even if that means sacrificing a good bottle of wine. I've included a foolproof recipe for making your own whenever you feel like it (*see* page 254).

• The butter Romans use is unsalted. You won't see it used often in this book because butter is more characteristic of the food of northern Italy, whereas from Tuscany down most recipes call for olive oil instead.

• Artichokes are the holy grail of Roman cuisine. Italian artichokes are small and violet, and have no discernible choke. Here is a stress-free way to clean them:

Cut a lemon in two and literally dip your fingertips in one half – this will prevent them from getting stained. Alternatively, wear disposable rubber gloves. Half fill a medium bowl with water and squeeze in the juice of the other half of the lemon. Snap off the tough green outer leaves of the artichoke, until you reach the tender yellow and violet leaves. Using a small sharp knife, cut off all but 4 cm ($1^1/_2$ inches) of the stem, then trim away the bright green skin from the base of the artichoke, using a spiral movement from the bottom to the top of the stem, until you get a rose shape. Cut off the top third of the artichoke – the pointy end. Brush the cut parts with lemon juice. If using large globe artichokes, you will need to remove the choke: grab the small, purple-tipped leaves at the centre of the artichoke and pull them out, then scrape out the choke, making sure not to leave any of the hairy, fuzzy bits behind. Place the artichoke in the bowl of acidulated water to stop it turning brown.

Chapter I BREAKFAST RITUAL AL BAR

I've always been an early riser. Early mornings in Rome seem to contain a languorous secret: you have the city to yourself and you can hear the sound of your steps on the *sanpietrini* – the Roman cobblestones. Laid in order to lead pilgrims towards the Vatican, they have been polished to a shine by millions of pious feet. The downside is that they can become quite slippery, making them unsuitable for high speeds or high heels. The cobblestones are perfect, however, for those serendipitous meetings with a handsome stranger: you think you're gliding elegantly but stumble instead, ending up in a heap on the ground together with your shopping bags and your self-esteem.

At sunrise a peculiar crowd inhabits the city: garbage collectors, street artists, revellers making their way home, but not before indulging at a coffee bar. Most Italians rarely consider breakfast a meal; they simply make a quick stop at a café on their way to work, where they drink their coffee standing up, *al bar*. It'd be hard to imagine Italy without coffee. In fact, you could say *caffè* is the national breakfast. All Italians are coffee connoisseurs, even the ones who aren't. First they pay whichever member of the café-owner's family is behind the till that morning, then they take the receipt to the counter and order their coffee. If the café has tables and chairs, the coffee you drink standing at the bar will cost much less than the one you drink sitting down.

But remember: when you order a *caffè* in Italy, it'll always means a *caffè espresso*. Do you fancy a change? Order a *caffè macchiato*, an espresso with a little bit of steamed milk in it, or a *caffè marocchino*, a macchiato with chocolate powder, or a *caffè Americano*, which is an espresso with a lot of hot water added to it. If you want more milk and more froth, order a *cappuccino*, but never ever after breakfast time or you'll get some weird looks. If, however, you want to breakfast like a true Roman ask the barista for '*cappuccio e cornetto*', a cappuccino and a croissant. Here the choices are endless: plain or with chocolate, filled with cream or jam. It could be a *bombolone* (the Italian version of a doughnut, *see* page 31), a cushiony *maritozzo* (*see* page 18) or a flaky *ventaglio* (*see* page 20) handed to you by the barista with a radiant smile. After that even the drabness of Monday morning won't look so bad.

STICKY BUNS

The *maritozzo* is the centrepiece of my Roman breakfast. With its curious name – an affectionate derivative of *marito*, which means husband – it's a tease in the form of a sticky bun. It first became popular in the Middle Ages as a token of love, when the girl who made the most scrumptious *maritozzo* would gain the most delectable honour of all: the attention of the most beautiful young man in the neighbourhood. Now, who wouldn't want to give that a go? Falling for such a deliciously tempting treat is as easy as falling in love for the first time.

Preparation time: 30 minutes plus rising

Cooking time: 20 minutes

Makes 8 *maritozzi*

1 teaspoon fast-action dried yeast

200ml (7fl oz) lukewarm water

1 teaspoon malt extract or caster sugar

375g (13oz) Canadian very strong white bread flour, plus extra if necessary

70g (2½oz) caster sugar

pinch of salt

70ml (2½fl oz) corn oil

zest of 1 lemon

2 eggs, separated

20g (¾oz) raisins, soaked in warm water for 10 minutes and drained

20g (¾oz) pine nuts

zest of 1 orange

Sugar Syrup:

120g (4 oz) white sugar

80ml water (2½fl oz)

Filling:

350ml (12fl oz) whipping cream

30g (1oz) icing sugar

50g (1¾oz) pistachios, crushed to a fine powder

Dissolve the yeast in 50ml (2fl oz) of the measured water, add the malt extract and mix well.

In a bowl, mix together the flour and sugar. Make a well in the centre, add the yeast and malt mixture and stir everything together.

In a separate bowl, add the salt, corn oil and lemon zest to the remaining water and stir together, then pour the liquid over the flour mixture, add the egg yolks and knead together to form a firm dough. Add the raisins, pine nuts and orange zest to the dough and continue to knead until all the ingredients are well combined.

Dust the dough and bowl with a little flour, cover with clingfilm and leave to rise in a warm place for at least 2 hours, or until it has risen by about one-third.

Transfer the risen dough onto a floured work surface and knead it for a couple of minutes, adding a little more flour if necessary, to obtain a firm and elastic dough. Divide the dough into eight pieces, then shape each piece into a round bun. Arrange the *maritozzi* on an oven tray lined with baking paper, cover with clingfilm and leave to rest for another 30 minutes.

Once the buns have rested, shape them into ovals and brush them with the egg white. Cover them again with clingfilm and leave them to rise for 1 hour.

While the *maritozzi* are rising, preheat the oven to 180°C (350°F), Gas Mark 4 and prepare the sugar syrup. Heat the sugar and water in a saucepan over a medium heat for 3–5 minutes without stirring until the liquid becomes transparent. Set aside to cool.

Bake the *maritozzi* for 20 minutes, or until golden brown, then remove them from the oven and brush with the sugar syrup. Leave them to cool on the tray for at least 20 minutes.

For the filling, whisk the cream together with the icing sugar until stiff peaks form. Make a cut lengthways along each *maritozzo* and fill each with the whipped cream and a sprinkle of crushed pistachios. Heaven in a bun.

Ventagli

FLAKY PASTRY FANS

As soon as May arrives, Rome becomes ragingly hot. In the past, when gentlemen sought to escape the oppressive heat at festivities dedicated to Bacchus, the Roman god of wine and intoxication, they would find a quiet spot to be fanned by pretty girls with ostrich feather fans. In the Renaissance era, fans were a staple of the female costume – Lucrezia Borgia apparently had a collection of them – and feathers, ivory and precious metals were the norm, tailor-made to satisfy any whim. Whatever the shape of the fan, it served as a tool of seduction during social events – when it was not being used as a fly swatter, of course.

Fragrant and sweet-scented, these lovely flaky fans are the epitome of Roman morning delights. Store them in an airtight container and they'll last for up to five days.

Preparation time: 10 minutes plus chilling

Cooking time: 20 minutes

Serves 6

1 x 320-g (11½-oz) all-butter puff pastry sheet, thawed if frozen

75g (2½oz) light brown sugar

zest of 1 lemon

75g (2½oz) caster sugar

Preheat the oven to 180°C (350°F), Gas Mark 4. Line an oven tray with greaseproof paper.

Unroll the puff pastry sheet and sprinkle over the brown sugar and lemon zest to coat the surface evenly.

Starting from one of the shorter sides, tightly roll the pastry into the middle, being careful not to tear it as you go. Repeat from the opposite side, leaving you with two adjoined tight pastry rolls. Loosely wrap the pastry in baking paper and place it in the freezer for 15 minutes to firm up (this will make it easier to cut).

After 15 minutes, remove the pastry from the freezer and cut it widthways into 1-cm (½-inch) slices. Tip the caster sugar into a bowl and dip each slice into it to ensure they are completely coated on both sides.

Arrange the pastry fans on the prepared oven tray, being sure to leave at least 2.5cm (1 inch) of space around each. Bake for 20 minutes, turning halfway, until golden brown and cooked through. Remove from the oven and leave to cool on a wire rack before serving.

GRANOLA

In a city of excess, where showgirls can be elected to parliament but the average graduate is lucky to get an underpaid job, you might sometimes feel that the world is going crazy and that you are surrounded by nutters. Don't worry – at least this granola is full of the good kind of nuts. What I love about this recipe is that you can tailor it to your own taste, using whatever dried fruit, nuts, or tasty bits take your fancy. This breakfast will give you a soft, yet energetic start to the day. Go nuts for the nuts.

Preparation time: 5 minutes plus soaking

Cooking time: 30 minutes

Makes about 850g (1lb 14oz)

100g (3½oz) raisins

130g (4½oz) whole almonds

100g (3½oz) pumpkin seeds

100g (3½oz) sunflower seeds

300g (10½oz) oat flakes

130g (4½oz) chopped dried apricots

50g (1¾oz) maple syrup

50g (1¾oz) clear wildflower honey

Preheat the oven to 150°C (300°F), Gas Mark 2. Line an oven tray with greaseproof paper.

Place the raisins in a small bowl of water and leave to soak for 30 minutes, then drain and squeeze them dry with your hands.

Mix the rest of the dry ingredients together in a bowl. Pour over the maple syrup and honey and mix everything together well.

Spread the granola out on the prepared tray in an even layer and bake for 30 minutes, giving the tray a shake every so often and adding the raisins halfway through cooking, until crisp and evenly browned.

Remove the tray from the oven and use the end of a rolling pin to break the granola up into bite-sized pieces. Leave to cool before storing in an airtight container for up to 15 days.

Treccia di brioche con scaglie di cioccolato

BRIOCHE BRAID WITH CHOCOLATE FLAKES

Rome is the city with the most churches in the world – on a bright, pristine morning you can spy their cupolas from rooftop terraces with views as far as the eye can see. The history of the dome has accompanied the city for 17 centuries, marking religious, social and artistic evolutions. Today, the central dome of St Peter's basilica still dominates the Roman horizon. The domes rising from this fabulously soft bread look like little cupolas. This breakfast delight takes some time to prepare, but its beauty is hard to beat, like the view on the threshold of another dimension.

Preparation time: 20 minutes plus rising

Cooking time: 25–30 minutes

Makes 1 x 900g (2lb) loaf

500g (1lb 2oz) strong white flour

1 teaspoon fast-action dried yeast

50g (1¾oz) caster sugar

4 eggs, beaten, plus 1 egg yolk

pinch of salt

6 cardamom pods, seeds extracted and ground

200g (7oz) unsalted butter, diced

50g (1¾oz) good-quality dark chocolate (70% cocoa solids), broken into roughly 1-cm (½-inch) squares

4 soft dried whole apricots, cut into quarters

2 tablespoons milk

3 teaspoons black poppy seeds

Line a 900g (2lb) loaf tin with baking paper.

Sift the flour, yeast and sugar into a large mixing bowl or the bowl of a stand mixer with the dough hook attachment added, tip in the beaten eggs and knead together for 15 minutes, adding the salt, cardamom and diced butter a little at a time, to form a firm yet elastic dough. Transfer the dough to a bowl, cover with clingfilm and leave to rise in a warm place for 2 hours, or until doubled in size.

Knock the air out of the dough by lightly smashing it with your hands until it is smooth, then divide it in half. Divide each half into eight equal-sized pieces, shape into balls and insert a square of chocolate and a quarter of an apricot into each, folding the dough around to make sure the filling is covered.

Arrange the dough balls in a tightly packed, even layer in the prepared loaf tin. Cover with aluminium foil and leave to rise for another 2 hours.

Preheat the oven to 180°C (350°F), Gas Mark 4.

Beat the egg yolk together with the milk and use it to brush over the surface of the bread. Sprinkle over the poppy seeds and bake for 25–30 minutes, until the loaf is lightly golden and sounds hollow when removed from the tin and tapped on the base. Leave the loaf to rest for 5 minutes, then remove it from the tin and leave to cool on a wire rack before serving.

Biscotti brutti ma buoni

UGLY BUT GOOD BISCUITS

If not all that glitters is gold, the opposite is also true. It is maddening how some of Italy's greatest gastronomic delights look paradoxically unappealing. Take these biscuits, for example, which resemble little mushy monsters. They are neither chromatically synchronized, nor are they balanced in terms of calorie versus fat intake. However, their colour reminds me of the generously fertile soil of my beloved Italy, and beauty is in the eye of the beholder, after all.

Preparation time: 20 minutes

Cooking time: 15 minutes

Makes 40 biscuits

80ml (2½fl oz) water

1 teaspoon clear honey

300g (10½oz) icing sugar

150g (5½oz) whole blanched hazelnuts

150g (5½oz) almonds

4 egg whites

pinch of salt

50g (1¾oz) pomegranate seeds

Preheat the oven to 180°C (350°F), Gas Mark 4. Line an oven tray with greaseproof baking paper.

Gently heat the measured water, honey and 50g (1¾oz) of the icing sugar in a small saucepan until the sugar has dissolved. Remove from the heat and let cool.

Tip half the hazelnuts and almonds into a food processor and whiz together briefly until coarsely chopped.

Whisk the egg whites together with the salt in a bowl, until stiff peaks form. Continue to whisk, gradually adding the cooled sugar syrup and the remaining icing sugar little by little for a further 10 minutes until glossy and firm.

Add the chopped nuts to the egg whites, folding them in gently with a metal spoon from bottom to top to prevent any air escaping. Fold in the remaining whole nuts.

Use two teaspoons to shape 2-cm (½-inch) balls of the mixture and arrange these on the lined oven tray in rows spaced 2cm (½ inch) apart. Sprinkle a few pomegranate seeds over each biscuit and bake for 15 minutes, until golden brown and crisp. Leave to cool and store in an airtight container for up to 10 days.

Bignè di San Giuseppe

ST JOSEPH'S DAY CREAM PUFFS

Around mid-March and throughout the Carnival season, all the *pasticcerie* in town announce the impending arrival of *il bignè di San Giuseppe*. The colour of the 'Golden Tiber', this fried puff pastry is filled with a thrilling cream that tastes like ambrosia. A cream-smudged nose and a satisfied soul will be the result of tasting these captivating delights. They call my name from the shop window, and I always buy more than I should. You can adapt this recipe to make *pastarelle*, which are made all year round – simply halve the size of each *bignè*.

Preparation time: 30 minutes plus cooling

Cooking time: 20-30 minutes

Makes about 10 *bignè*

170ml (6fl oz) milk

170ml (6fl oz) water

100g (3½oz) unsalted butter, softened and diced

1 teaspoon caster sugar

1 teaspoon salt

170g (6oz) plain flour

zest of 1 orange

2 eggs

vegetable oil, for frying (optional)

100g (3½oz) icing sugar

Custard:

6 tablespoons caster sugar

6 egg yolks

720ml (1¼ pints) milk

6 tablespoons plain flour

zest of 1 lemon

Icing:

3 tablespoons water

100g (3½oz) icing sugar, sifted

dash of pink, yellow or blue food colouring (optional)

For the custard, mix together the sugar and egg yolks in a saucepan, then add the milk, flour and lemon zest. Heat gently, stirring continuously, until the mixture starts to bubble, then continue to simmer for 2–3 minutes. Transfer to a bowl and leave to cool. Cover with clingfilm and set aside.

In a heavy-based saucepan, stir together the milk, measured water, butter, sugar and salt over a medium-low heat. Cook, stirring, for 1–2 minutes until the mixture is thick and creamy. Add the sifted flour and orange zest and stir quickly and continuously to form a smooth ball of dough that comes away from the sides of the pan. Tip the dough into a bowl and leave to cool for 10 minutes before beating in the eggs.

Cut a 24 x 18-cm (9½ x 7-inch) rectangle of greaseproof paper into squares. Using two tablespoons or a piping bag, form round fig-sized mounds of the pastry on top of each square.

To fry the *bignè*, half-fill a large pot or deep-fryer with vegetable oil and heat to 180°C (350°F), or until a cube of bread browns in 30 seconds. Carefully lower the *bignè*, each still attached to its paper square (these will come off after a few seconds and can be removed with tongs) into the hot oil and fry for 1–2 minutes until golden on all sides. Remove the pastries with a slotted spoon and drain them on a plate lined with kitchen paper, then cover them with the icing sugar.

Alternatively, for a healthier version, preheat the oven to 180°C (350°F), Gas Mark 4. Arrange the *bignè* on their paper squares on an oven tray, cover them with icing sugar and bake for about 25 minutes, until golden.

Once the pastries have cooked and cooled, carefully make a hole at the bottom of each. Use a piping bag to fill the *bignè* with the custard.

For the icing, bring the measured water to a boil in a small saucepan and add the icing sugar a tablespoon at a time, stirring constantly to dissolve, until the mix is smooth and all the sugar has been incorporated. For a coloured glaze, add a few drops of food colouring to the mix.

Smear the top of each *bignè* with a teaspoon or so of the icing and refrigerate until ready to serve.

Bomboloni

BAKED DOUGHNUTS

As a child, I used to be a doughnut queen, slipping them on my fingers as symbols of my power (the power of being a pest!). Now that I'm a grown-up, well most of the time, I like to let the aroma of freshly baked doughnuts float me into consciousness, reassuring me that all is well with the world as I wake up. A little voluptuous recklessness, and I'm ready for the day ahead. In this recipe I use mashed potato flakes in order to create an extra-moist doughnut. If you don't have instant mashed potato in your cupboard, you can substitute the real thing instead.

Preparation time: 20 minutes plus rising

Cooking time: 15 minutes

Makes 20 *bomboloni*

200ml (1/3 pint) milk

75g (2 1/2oz) instant mashed potato flakes

1 teaspoon fast-action dried yeast

250g (9oz) plain flour, plus extra for dusting

250g (9oz) Canadian very strong white bread flour

3 eggs, plus 1 beaten egg yolk for brushing

85g (3oz) caster sugar, plus extra for dusting

85g (3oz) softened unsalted butter, plus extra for brushing

zest of 1 orange

zest of 1 lemon

Line a baking tray with baking paper.

In a small bowl, mix together 150ml (1/4 pint) of milk with the potato flakes until thick and creamy.

In a separate bowl, dissolve the yeast in the remaining milk.

Sift the flours into a large mixing bowl or the bowl of a stand mixer with the dough hook attachment added and add the potato mix, yeast mix and all the remaining ingredients. Knead for 15 minutes to form a soft dough that comes away from the sides of the bowl.

Place the dough in a large bowl, cover with a clean tea towel and set aside in a warm place to prove for 2–3 hours, or until the dough has tripled in size.

Roll the dough out on a lightly floured work surface to a 1-cm (1/2-inch) thickness. Using a 9-cm (3 1/2-inch) floured doughnut cutter, cut out 20 doughnuts. Alternatively, if you don't have a doughnut cutter, try using the rim of a tumbler, flouring it as you go, to cut out 20 circles, then use the rim of a regular shot glass to remove the dough from the centre of each circle to form the holes.

Carefully place the doughnuts on the prepared baking tray, making sure to leave at least 2.5cm (1 inch) between them. Cover the doughnuts with a tea towel and leave to prove for a further 30 minutes.

Preheat the oven to 180°C (350°F), Gas Mark 4.

Brush the proved doughnuts with egg wash and bake for 10–15 minutes until golden. Remove from the oven and brush with a little melted butter, then dust generously with sugar. Serve warm or cold.

Biscottoni da inzuppo

DUNKING BISCUITS

Although I didn't know it at the time, it was in my grandmother's pantry, that exuberant temple of gluttony, that a sort of initiation to what would become an existence of utter gratification through the joys of food first occurred. Moist, nutty and simple, these exquisite biscuits hold all the nostalgic splendour that I associate with childhood. I love to dip them in my cappuccino or crumble them over plain yogurt in the morning. And wherever I am in the world, whenever I taste a biscuit echoing with this aroma, I know I'm home.

Preparation time: 15 minutes plus cooling

Cooking time: 20–25 minutes

Makes 30 biscuits

butter, for greasing

500g (1lb 2oz) super-fine grade 00 pasta flour, plus extra for dusting

1 teaspoon bicarbonate of soda

1 teaspoon cream of tartar

250g (9oz) caster sugar, plus 30g (1oz) extra for dusting

3 large eggs, plus 1 beaten egg for brushing

125ml (4fl oz) milk

1/2 teaspoon baking powder

100ml (3 1/2fl oz) extra virgin olive oil

Preheat the oven to 180°C (350°F), Gas Mark 4. Grease a large ladyfinger biscuit mould or a baking tray with butter and dust it with flour.

Put the flour in a bowl with the bicarbonate of soda, cream of tartar and sugar. Crack in the eggs and whisk together until pale and fluffy.

Gently warm the milk in a saucepan, then remove from the heat, add the baking powder and stir to dissolve. Tip the warm milk into the egg mix and stir to combine before adding the oil and working everything together to form a wet, spongy dough.

Fill the prepared biscuit mould with the dough, gently pressing and patting the dough into each mould to ensure a neat shape. Alternatively, use a piping bag to pipe the dough onto the baking tray in 10 x 2-cm (4 x 3/4-inch) rectangles, leaving at least 1cm (1/2 inch) between each piece. Brush with the beaten egg and bake for 10–15 minutes. Remove from the oven and sprinkle with caster sugar, then bake for a further 5–10 minutes until the biscuits are golden on top and firm to the touch. Leave to cool on a wire rack for at least 30 minutes, preferably overnight, before storing in an airtight container for up to 2 months. Serve with coffee or cold milk for dunking.

Fette biscottate

SWEET MELBA TOAST

There are times – especially when I'm trying to stick to my New Year's resolutions – when I allow myself fewer treats, but these crackling toasts are always among them. These irresistible golden crisps find their perfect match in homemade seasonal jam, but I also enjoy them more ascetically, just on their own, without all the colourful clamour that I usually associate with Rome.

Preparation time: 15 minutes plus rising

Cooking time: 1³/4 hours

Makes 15–20 toasts

150g (5¹/2oz) softened unsalted butter, plus extra for greasing

125ml (4fl oz) milk

1 x 7-g (¹/4-oz) sachet fast-action dried yeast

20g (³/4oz) brown sugar

120ml (4fl oz) lukewarm water

500g (1lb 2oz) Canadian very strong white bread flour

3 large eggs, plus 1 beaten egg for brushing

1 teaspoon salt

50g (1³/4oz) flaxseed

Butter and line a 23-cm (9-inch) loaf tin with greaseproof paper. In a small pan, warm the milk gently until lukewarm.

Add the yeast and half the sugar to the measured water in a bowl and stir together to dissolve.

Sift the flour into a separate bowl or the bowl of a stand mixer with the dough hook attachment added. Making a well in the centre, add the dissolved yeast mixture, eggs, remaining sugar and warm milk. Knead well for about 10 minutes to form a smooth, elastic dough, then add the salt, flaxseed and softened butter little by little until it is fully incorporated. Knead for a further 5 minutes. Roll the dough into a ball, cover the bowl with a clean tea towel and leave to rise in a warm place for 45 minutes, or until doubled in size.

Taking the dough with your hands, shape it to roughly the size of the prepared loaf tin. Gently lower the dough into the tin and leave it to rise for a further 1 hour. Don't worry about the dough overhanging the tin, it will make for beautifully shaped toasts.

Preheat the oven to 180°C (350°F), Gas Mark 4.

Brush the dough with the last beaten egg and bake for 45 minutes, or until the loaf is lightly golden and sounds hollow when removed from the tin and tapped on the base. Remove the loaf from the tin and leave to cool on a wire rack for 1 hour.

Once cool, slice the loaf into roughly 1-cm (¹/2-inch) pieces – you can slice them thicker or thinner depending on personal taste. Arrange the slices on a baking tray covered with baking paper and bake at 150°C (300°F), Gas Mark 2 for a further 1 hour, at the end of which they'll be dry and golden. Leave the toasts to cool on a wire rack before storing in an airtight container, where they will last for up to 1 week.

Budini di riso

RICE PUDDING TARTLETS

Trastevere, where I got this recipe, is the undisputed street food centre of Rome. It is also home to the most outspoken Roman *matrone*, who treat each meal with a solemn sense of ceremony. The true food connoisseur knows that these formidable Roman women were dictating food trends when celebrity chefs were still in nappies. They would never go to a supermarket filled with convenience foods – you'll only find them shopping at the local market, spreading their unshakable opinions on today's customs. 'EAT!' they command if you sit at their table. That's how I grew up, and why I made it a rule to go jogging twice a week. These tartlets are full of Italian *mamma* warmth and spiky charm. Wait until the rice turns translucent and creamy, then pour it into the pastry shells. This dish is like the Romans: a bit hard on the outside, but with a tremendous amount of heart.

Preparation time: 15 minutes plus chilling

Cooking time: 60 minutes

Makes 12 tartlets

1 litre (1¾ pints) milk

zest of 1 lemon

1 tablespoon vanilla extract or 1 vanilla pod, split lengthways and seeds scraped

300g (10½oz) carnaroli or arborio risotto rice

6 tablespoons light brown sugar

2 teaspoons baking powder

2 large eggs, separated

pinch of salt

Pastry:

100g (3½oz) plain flour

100g (3½oz) wholegrain spelt flour

100g (3½oz) rice flour

100g (3½oz) demerara sugar

pinch of salt

2 teaspoons baking powder

150g (5½oz) cold unsalted butter, diced

1 large egg

Line the holes of a 12-cup muffin tray with baking paper.

For the pastry. sift the three flours into a large bowl and mix together with the sugar, salt and baking powder. Add the butter and stir together with a wooden spoon to form a crumbly dough. (Try not to touch the butter with your hands as it will melt, making for a soggy pastry.)

Beat the egg in a bowl, add it to the dough and mix everything together until smooth. Roll the dough into a ball, wrap it in clingfilm and let it rest in the refrigerator for 1 hour.

Pour the milk into a large heavy-based saucepan, add the lemon zest and vanilla extract or seeds and bring to a simmer. When it starts bubbling, add the rice and cook for 20–30 minutes, or according to packet instructions, until the rice is soft and creamy. Remove from the heat, add half the brown sugar and leave to cool.

Preheat the oven to 170°C (340°F), Gas Mark 3.

When the rice has cooled completely, stir in the baking powder, egg yolks and remaining sugar.

In a separate bowl, whip the egg whites with a pinch of salt until firm, then fold them delicately into the rice pudding.

Divide the dough into 12 equal-sized pieces. Taking one piece, gently press the pastry with your fingers into one of the prepared muffin cups. Repeat with the remaining pastry pieces.

Spoon the rice pudding into the pastry shells and bake until the rice tartlets are golden brown around the edges, about 40 minutes. Remove from the oven and serve warm or cold, with a dusting of icing sugar or some fresh fruit and yogurt.

Chapter 2 MERENDE

'Che ne voi artri du' chicchetti?' – 'Why don't you have a couple more mouthfuls?' was the question those tall women piously dressed in black would always ask in the canteen of my Catholic elementary school. The nun who introduced me to a love for everything that smells good and tastes comforting was called Suor Fortunata. An abundance of flesh, eau de Cologne and sweets were her particular traits, along with a liberal use of guilt as an educational tool. When school was out for the summer, I would hop on a coach filled with screaming children. Destination: summer camp. This would usually be held in one of the many medieval monasteries dotted around the Roman countryside, and yet it would always take no less than 4 hours to get there. Was it the magic of the packed school bus or the voice of Suor Beata (Blessed Sister – could you ever compete with that ethereal grace?) reverberating with flinty humour that slowed time down to a crawl? I couldn't tell.

In the afternoons, we would furtively run to the pantry to indulge in some crunchy *ovis molis* (*see* page 57) or *pizzette rosse* (*see* page 55). As soon as a nun arrived, however, we would hide behind the extra-large jar filled with *tarallucci* (*see* page 43), since we knew that anyone caught helping themselves to a *merenda* or snack before dinner time, thereby violating the sanctity of the meal, would be in big trouble.

Everyone had to help prepare the evening meal: one of us would peel the potatoes, another would crack eggs into a dish to prepare the *costolette* (breaded veal chops). This ritual, which I now habitually re-create in my own life by enlisting the help of friends and family in the kitchen, was a sort of sumptuous confessional. The handling of all this food punctuated our personalities, which emerged through telling stories and cracking jokes. It created intimacy.

Those sweet-tempered, indefatigable, often moustachioed women taught me how to recognize the best produce and to respect every season. Many churches in Rome and beyond still boast a *hortum botanicum*, a lovingly tended vegetable garden, the congregation's pride and joy, which according to the season provides a bountiful supply of cabbages, tomatoes, chicory, radishes, aubergines, potatoes, peppers and more.

Tarallucci al vino

BAKED SWEET WINE PRETZELS

The walls of Fiaschetteria Beltramme, a restaurant on Via della Croce, are lined with rows of 19th-century *fiaschi* – traditional straw-wrapped wine bottles. The villages of the Castelli Romani area, from Ariccia, where *porchetta* (*see* page 188) comes from, to Tivoli, home to the splendid Villa Adriana, all have one thing in common: their soft, unfussy wine. What bliss to have your drink served with these crisp, wine-flavoured little snacks!
Tarallucci are also a perfect mood raiser for your mid-morning coffee break. They are traditionally made with sambuca (*see* page 271) and the kind of wine everyone despises because 'you can taste the cork'. This recipe is a perfect way to put it to good use, as throwing it away would be a sin in Italian *cucina povera* culture, where nothing is wasted.

Preparation time: 20 minutes

Cooking time: 20 minutes

Makes 40 *tarallucci*

350g (12oz) plain flour, plus extra for dusting

pinch of salt

2 tablespoons anise seeds

120ml (4fl oz) extra virgin olive oil

200g (3½oz) light brown sugar, plus extra for glazing

120ml (4fl oz) red wine

1 tablespoon Roman-style Sambuca (*see* page 271), Grand Marnier or other herb-based liqueur

Preheat the oven to 180°C (350°F), Gas Mark 4. Line a large baking tray with baking paper.

Put the flour, salt, anise seeds, oil and half the sugar into a bowl and mix together well. Gradually add the wine and sambuca and keep mixing to form a firm dough.

Divide the dough into 40 equal-sized pieces. Take a piece and shape it into a ball, then, using the palms of your hands, roll it out on a floured surface into a thin rope about 10cm (4 inches) long. Bring the ends together to form a ring (don't worry if it isn't quite a perfect circle – it's fine if it looks more like a teardrop). Repeat with the rest of the dough pieces.

Put the remaining brown sugar into a bowl and dip the dough rings in to coat them completely. Arrange the *tarallucci* on the prepared baking tray, leaving 1cm (½ inch) between them, and bake for 20 minutes or until golden brown.

Let the *tarallucci* cool on a wire rack for 2 hours before serving.

Insalata di farro con pollo, zucchine e formaggio di capra

SPELT SALAD WITH CHICKEN, COURGETTES & GOATS' CHEESE

When I put my New Year's resolutions into practice, I start the day with a cup of hot water and lemon juice. Later on I make this wonderfully light, tasty recipe that catches the flavours of my Rome. Not that I should be feeling smug, because this is incredibly quick and easy. With a delicious nutty taste, spelt is easier to digest than more common types of wheat. This dish is therefore also perfect for a date, since no one wants to be romantic on a heavy stomach. This recipe is just a starting point: feel free to use any ingredients that take your fancy.

Preparation time: 10 minutes plus soaking

Cooking time: 25 minutes

Serves 2

30g (1oz) raisins

150g (5^1/$_2$oz) pearled spelt or pearl barley

small handful of sea salt flakes

4 tablespoons extra virgin olive oil

100g (3^1/$_2$oz) chicken breast, cut into 1-cm (^{1}/$_2$-inch) strips

1 courgette, halved lengthways and very finely sliced

8 cherry tomatoes, cut into 5-mm (^{1}/$_4$-inch) cubes

100g (3^1/$_2$oz) semi-soft goats' cheese, cut into 5-mm (^{1}/$_4$-inch) cubes

100g (3^1/$_2$oz) rocket leaves, coarsely chopped

zest and juice of 1 lemon

small handful of chopped mint leaves

Place the raisins in a small bowl of water and leave to soak for 30 minutes, then drain and squeeze them dry with your hands.

Place the spelt in a large saucepan, cover with water and bring to a boil. Add the sea salt flakes and cook according to the package instructions until the spelt is fluffy but still retains a bit of crunch (this usually takes about 15–18 minutes). Once cooked, drain the spelt and pass it under cold running water to cool it and stop it cooking further. Transfer to a large bowl and set aside.

Heat 1 tablespoon of olive oil in a griddle pan or non-stick frying pan until smoking hot, then add the chicken and courgette strips and cook for 3 minutes on each side, brushing with the oil as you go, until the chicken is cooked through. Remove from the heat and set aside.

Add the tomatoes, goats' cheese, raisins and rocket leaves to the spelt. Drizzle over the remaining 3 tablespoons of olive oil and season with salt, then sprinkle over the lemon zest and squeeze over the lemon juice. Add the mint leaves and mix together well so that everything is evenly coated in the dressing. Pile the chicken and courgette strips on top of the salad and serve.

Trio di bruschette

THREE BRUSCHETTE OF A KIND

Literally meaning 'roasted', *bruschetta* is how farmers traditionally savoured bread – rubbed with garlic and seasoned with olive oil and salt. I love this dish: it puts me back in touch with the most authentic part of me. Each season has its own favourite topping combination, so get ready to free your imagination and enjoy the intensity of these mouth-watering morsels!

Preparation time: 10 minutes

Cooking time: 25 minutes

Makes 15 *bruschette*

1 rustic bread loaf, cut into 1-cm
(1/2-inch) thick slices

20 Marinated Anchovies or
Sardines (*see* page 147)

Tomato and aubergine topping:

2 tablespoons extra virgin olive oil

1 garlic clove, peeled and left whole

1 small aubergine, cut into 5-mm
(1/4-inch) chunks

2 cherry tomatoes, cut into 5-mm
(1/4-inch) chunks

50ml (2fl oz) white wine

5 sage leaves, chopped

salt

**Sausage and tenderstem broccoli
topping:**

1 pork sausage

80g (3oz) tenderstem broccoli
florets

2 tablespoons extra virgin olive oil

1 teaspoon fennel seeds

For the tomato and aubergine topping, heat the oil in a non-stick frying pan. Lightly crush the garlic clove with the side of a heavy knife, add to the pan and fry it gently until golden. Remove the garlic clove from the pan, add the aubergine and tomato pieces and season with salt. Increase the heat to medium-high, pour over the wine and cook, stirring, until the wine has evaporated and the aubergine is tender, about 10 minutes. Sprinkle over the sage leaves and set aside.

For the sausage and broccoli topping, squeeze the sausage out of its casing and cook in a small non-stick frying pan, breaking it up with a wooden spoon and stirring occasionally to prevent it catching on the dry pan, until cooked through. Bring a small pan of salted water to a boil, add the broccoli and cook for 5 minutes, then drain and transfer to the pan with the sausage. Add the oil and fennel seeds and continue to cook, stirring, for 5 minutes, to allow the flavours to mingle. Set aside.

Preheat the grill to medium–high.

Arrange the bread slices on an oven tray and place under the grill for 5 minutes until lightly golden. Transfer to a serving plate and divide the tomato and aubergine, the sausage and broccoli, and the marinated anchovy or sardine toppings evenly between the slices. Enjoy.

Torta rustica carciofi, piselli e prosciutto

SAVOURY PIE WITH ARTICHOKES, PEAS & HAM

White bread has always been associated with wealth, whereas dark bread was typical of simple country living. In 1870, a wave of country dwellers moved to Rome, Italy's newly elected capital. Wholemeal bread went out of fashion, as people tried to emulate the lifestyle of the upper classes. But food trends are cyclical, so this humble dish is back in the spotlight. This fabulously healthy pie is what I turn to when an unexpected craving hits me in the middle of the day. And no, you can't have too much of this good thing.

Preparation time: 15 minutes plus chilling

Cooking time: 1¼ hours

Serves 8

3 tablespoons extra virgin olive oil, plus extra for brushing

1 garlic clove, peeled and left whole

3 artichokes, cleaned (*see* page 13), quartered lengthways and placed in acidulated water

150g (5½oz) garden peas, defrosted if frozen

small handful of mint leaves, finely sliced

2 tablespoons water

400g (14oz) *mozzarella da cucina* (cooking mozzarella)

4 tablespoons breadcrumbs (*see* page 262)

200g (7oz) roast ham, cut into 3-mm (⅛-inch) strips

salt

Pastry:

200g (7oz) strong white flour

200g (7oz) rye flour

4 tablespoons white wine

pinch of salt

approx. 4 tablespoons water

small handful of basil leaves

For the pastry, stir together the flours, wine and salt in a large bowl together with enough water (about 4 tablespoons) to form a sticky dough. Add the basil and continue to mix together until smooth. Place the dough in a bowl, cover with a tea towel and leave to rest in the refrigerator for 30 minutes.

Preheat the oven to 180°C (350°F), Gas Mark 4.

Heat the oil in a large non-stick frying pan, add the garlic clove and fry it gently until it starts to brown, then remove it from the pan. Add the artichokes and peas and cook over a medium heat for 15 minutes until the vegetables have softened, adding the mint and water halfway through cooking. Season to taste and set aside.

Cut the mozzarella into roughly 1-cm (½-inch) cubes and pat them dry with kitchen paper to remove any excess water. Mix the mozzarella pieces together with the breadcrumbs to coat evenly.

Once chilled, roll three-quarters of the dough out with a rolling pin to a 5-mm (¼-inch) thickness. Cut out a 28-cm (11-inch) pastry disc to be placed on the base of a 25-cm (10-inch) pie dish, leaving the excess overhanging. Cut the remaining dough into seven 4-cm (1½-inch) wide strips.

Prick the base of the pie with a fork, then cover it with the ham, artichokes, peas, and crumbed mozzarella pieces. Arrange the pastry strips across the surface in a criss-cross lattice pattern, fold in the overhanging dough and seal the edges well. Brush with a little oil, cover with a sheet of baking paper and bake for 30 minutes. Remove the baking paper and bake for a further 30 minutes until the pastry is nicely golden. Enjoy hot or cold with a green salad or alongside a bowl of soup.

Tortino di verdure incartato

WRAPPED VEGETABLE PIE

With its exhilarating aroma and vivid flavour this is not your usual lasagne – instead of layers of egg pasta, here we use crunchy leaves of chard, giving this dish the appearance of a beautifully wrapped present. To me, herbs make up the personality traits of a dish. I like to use sage and basil here, but you can personalize this bewitching pie with any herb you fancy. Go on, make it yours.

Preparation time: 40 minutes

Cooking time: 1 hour 40 minutes

Serves 6

50g (1³/₄oz) salted butter

500g (1lb 2oz) leeks, trimmed, cleaned and finely sliced

handful of basil leaves, roughly chopped

handful of sage leaves, roughly chopped

500g (1lb 2oz) chard, trimmed and stalks separated

3 eggs

200ml (¹/₃ pint) whipping cream

1 carrot, cut into 5-mm (¹/₄-inch) cubes

1 celery stick, cut into 5-mm (¹/₄-inch) cubes

200g (7oz) radishes

salt and pepper

Melt the butter in a large saucepan over a very low heat, add the leeks and cook gently, stirring occasionally, for 1 hour, until the leeks are soft, translucent and falling apart. Stir in the basil and sage, season with salt and pepper and remove from the heat. Set aside.

Meanwhile, put the chard pieces into a large pan of salted boiling water and blanch for 2–3 minutes. Drain and let dry between two clean tea towels.

Preheat the oven to 180°C (350°F), Gas Mark 4. Dampen a sheet of baking paper with a little water and use to line an 18-cm (7-inch) springform cake tin.

In a bowl, beat the eggs together until light and fluffy. Add the whipping cream and beat together until the mixture is slightly firm, then season with salt and pepper and stir in the sautéed leeks along with the carrot and celery pieces.

Arrange the dried chard pieces, reserving a handful, in an overlapping pattern to cover the base and sides of the prepared cake tin. Fill the tin with the cream and vegetable mixture, then cover with the remaining leaves, folding the overhanging leaves towards the middle like a parcel to enclose the filling. Loosely cover the *tortino* with baking paper, and cook in the oven for 40 minutes until the filling has set firm.

Remove the *tortino* from the oven and gently flip it over, removing the baking paper. Using a mandoline or sharp knife, cut the radishes into thin slices and use to decorate the top of the *tortino*. Serve hot or cold.

MINI PIZZAS WITH TOMATO SAUCE

When it comes to the constant movie that is Rome, I like to take it in with all my senses alert. I'll take some *pizzette rosse* with me for my mid-morning stroll around the market while secretly people-watching. Eating while shopping for food: how very Roman! These fragrant beauties are even more delicious eaten the next day. Just warm them up in the oven at 110°C (225°F), Gas Mark ¼ for five minutes for some comfort food at its tastiest. I like to use a tiny espresso cup as a template for my mini pizzas, but you can also use a cappuccino cup or a cereal bowl for a larger pizza thrill.

Preparation time: 10 minutes plus rising

Cooking time: 15-20 minutes

Makes about 40 *pizzette*

250g (9oz) passata (sieved tomatoes)

small handful of basil leaves, chopped

2 tablespoons extra virgin olive oil

1 teaspoon salt

100g (3½oz) *mozzarella da cucina* (cooking mozzarella), cut into 5-mm (¼-inch) cubes

Dough:

500g (1lb 2oz) strong white flour, plus extra for dusting

1 teaspoon caster sugar

2 tablespoons fast-action dried yeast

250ml (9fl oz) lukewarm water plus 50ml (2fl oz)

30g (1oz) unsalted butter, softened

1 teaspoon extra virgin olive oil

1 teaspoon salt

To prepare the dough, sift the flour into a large mixing bowl with the sugar. Dissolve the yeast in 250ml (9fl oz) of lukewarm water, add it to the flour and sugar and mix together for 5 minutes. Add the butter, oil and salt and mix for a further 2–3 minutes to form a soft, sticky dough. Add up to 50ml (2fl oz) more water as needed – the dough should feel neither sticky nor dry. Cover the bowl with a clean tea towel and leave to rise in a warm place for 1 hour, or until almost doubled in size.

Preheat the oven to 200°C (400°F), Gas Mark 6. Mix the passata, basil, oil and salt together in a bowl and set aside.

To make the *pizzette*, roll out the risen dough on a clean, floured surface to a 1-cm (½-inch) thickness. Press down onto the surface of the dough with a small cup or glass of your choice to form your pizzette circles. Spoon a little of the passata over the centre of each *pizzetta*, being sure to leave the edges empty so that you have that typical white/red contrast of a good margherita.

Cook in the oven for 15–20 minutes, adding a few mozzarella cubes to the top of each *pizzetta* halfway through cooking, until the cheese is bubbling and the *pizzetta* bases are crisp. Enjoy.

Girelle di pan carrè con mousse di prosciutto cotto agrumata

SANDWICH WHEELS WITH PROSCIUTTO MOUSSE

At art gallery openings in Rome, you can see people's eyes flicking towards the buffet during the speeches. Don't be fooled by their perfectly pressed suits and glamorous hairdos, their only real interest lies in eating as much free food as possible.

To enjoy this prosciutto mousse at its best, be sure to prepare it at least 12 hours before serving. As with everything in life, organization is key. That's why cooking, to me, is like therapy: when life gets tough, I can start with the tiny details in the kitchen. If I can be organized there, then there's hope for everything else.

Preparation time: 30 minutes plus chilling

Serves 20 as part of a canapé selection

2 fine gelatine leaves

120ml (4fl oz) whipping cream

600g (1lb 2oz) smoked or roast ham, cut into 1-cm (¼-inch) cubes

2 tablespoons French mustard

2 tablespoons tomato ketchup

15 black peppercorns

4 tablespoons lemon juice

4 lemons

1 sliced white bread loaf

1 sliced wholemeal bread loaf

Soak the gelatine leaves in a small bowl of lukewarm water for 5 minutes, then remove and squeeze out the excess water.

Bring a medium-sized saucepan half filled with water to a simmer. Whisk together the whipping cream and gelatine leaves in an ovenproof bowl that fits snugly over the pan until the gelatine has dissolved. Set aside over a very low heat.

Put 500g (1lb 2oz) of the ham cubes into a food processor together with the mustard, ketchup, peppercorns and lemon juice and blend together for 30 seconds to form a light, creamy paste. Add the warm cream and gelatine mixture and blend together for a further 30 seconds, then spoon the mousse into a large bowl and fold in the remaining ham cubes.

Wet a 16-cm (6¼-inch) square terrine mould under running water, then line it with a sheet of baking paper. Fill the mould with the mousse, cover it with clingfilm and leave it to chill and set for at least 12 hours, preferably overnight.

When you're ready to serve, halve the lemons and slice the halves as thinly as possible. Remove the crust from the bread slices and cut each slice into four pieces.

Spread a generous amount of the mousse on a bread slice quarter and roll it up into a coil. Place a slice of lemon on top of the rolled slice and skewer it with a cocktail stick to fix it in place. Repeat with the remaining ingredients, and arrange the sandwich wheels on a large serving platter to finish. Serve alongside a range of other nibbles (*see* pages 126–49).

Trio di ovis molis alle marmellate

SHORTBREAD BISCUIT TRIO WITH JAM

The nuns at my school evangelized about a simpler way of life, where the only appropriate activities were prayer and tending the vegetable garden. *Ora et labora*. They would regularly pick the ingredients they needed in their kitchen garden – a cook's idea of heaven.
The best flavour combinations come from ingredients that grow together, so during jam-making season, peaches, apricots and strawberries would make for a happy bunch. This trio of biscuits makes my soul sparkle – the colours of the different types of jam, the icing sugar sprinkled over the top and the soothing taste all combine to ensure great satisfaction.

Preparation time: 5 minutes plus cooling

Cooking time: 15 minutes

Makes about 20 biscuits

50g (1³/₄oz) sunflower seeds

100g (3¹/₂oz) strong white flour

50g (1³/₄oz) icing sugar, plus extra for dusting

80g (3oz) cold unsalted butter, diced

zest of 1 lemon

1 egg yolk

¹/₂ teaspoon baking powder

1 tablespoon each of your 3 favourite jams (I like apricot, peach and strawberry)

20 raspberries (optional)

Preheat the oven to 180°C (350°F), Gas Mark 4. Line an oven tray with greaseproof paper.

Tip the sunflower seeds into a clean coffee or spice grinder and grind to a fine powder.

Sift the flour into a bowl, add the icing sugar, ground sunflower seeds, butter, lemon zest, egg yolk and baking powder and mix everything together well to form a firm dough.

Divide the dough into 20 equal-sized balls. Using your thumb, press down on the centre of each ball to create a dimple.

Arrange the biscuits on the prepared tray and bake for 12 minutes until the biscuits are slightly golden. Remove the biscuits from the oven and leave them to cool on a wire rack.

Meanwhile, gently heat your chosen jams in 3 separate small pans until liquid in consistency.

Once the biscuits have cooled, spoon a little of your first hot jam into the dimples of a third of the biscuits. Repeat with the remaining jams and biscuits. Top each biscuit with a raspberry, if you like, and sprinkle with icing sugar to finish.

Ciambellone di polenta alla zucca e mele

POLENTA CAKE WITH PUMPKIN & APPLE

Rome is built on seven hills: Campidoglio, Celio, Esquilino, Palatino, Viminale, Quirinale and Aventino. This last hill is the quieter one, with a solemn air. It also has an ace in the hole that I like to keep as a surprise when strolling through the city with non-Roman friends – the keyhole of the gate to the Priory of the Knights of Malta. Peep through it and you will enjoy a spellbinding view of the dome of St Peter's, framed by the orange trees in the priory garden. This cake bursts with so much flavour that I can't help but be taken back to that magnificent garden in the summer, when the air is pervaded by the heady scent of ripe oranges. In this recipe, the polenta mixed together with earthy orange pumpkin purée and apples makes for a vibrant combination. Dizzyingly delicious.

Preparation time: 10 minutes plus soaking and cooling

Cooking time: 1 hour 50 minutes

Serves 10

unsalted butter, for greasing

500g (1lb 2oz) plain flour, plus extra for dusting

150g (5½oz) raisins

400g (14oz) peeled pumpkin, cut into 5-cm (2-inch) cubes

2 Bramley or other cooking apples, peeled, cored and diced

4 large eggs

400g (14oz) caster sugar

4 tablespoons extra virgin olive oil

150g (5½oz) polenta (cornmeal) flour

2 teaspoons baking powder

1 tablespoon rum

zest of 1 orange

250g (9oz) redcurrants

icing sugar, to decorate

Preheat the oven to 200°C (400°F), Gas Mark 6. Line an oven tray with greaseproof paper and grease a 32cm (13 inch) springform cake tin or savarin ring mould and dust it with flour.

Place the raisins in a small bowl of water and leave to soak for 30 minutes, then drain and squeeze them dry with your hands.

Meanwhile, arrange the pumpkin pieces on the prepared oven tray and bake for 40 minutes, or until soft. Remove from the oven and leave to cool for 10 minutes, then crush the pumpkin pieces with a fork to a rough purée-like consistency.

Tip the apple pieces into a saucepan, cover with water and bring to a simmer. Cook over a medium heat for about 10 minutes, until the apple pieces are soft and just starting to break down. Drain and set aside.

Whisk the eggs together with the sugar in a large bowl until pale and fluffy. Whisking continuously, gradually add the oil, then sift over the flours and baking powder and mix together to form a batter. Add the rum, raisins and orange zest, followed by the pumpkin and apple, and mix everything together well.

Gently fill the prepared cake tin with the cake batter and bake in the oven for 10 minutes. Reduce the heat to 170°C (340°F), Gas Mark 3 and cook for a further 50 minutes, until the cake is lightly golden, the sides are coming away from the edges of the tin and a cake tester inserted into the middle of the cake comes out clean.

Remove from the tin and leave to cool on a wire rack. Decorate the top of the cake with sprigs of redcurrants and dust with icing sugar before serving.

WHEAT & CANDIED FRUIT CAKE

Suor Serena, my favourite nun, has a particular love for *Tosca*. As the opera's protagonist awaits his execution, we hear a melancholy aria: 'The stars were shining, the earth was fragrant, the garden gate creaked, and a footstep brushed the sand. She entered, fragrant, and fell into my arms. And I've never loved life as much.' To Suor Serena, this song resembles the preparation of *pastiera*: the combination of cooked wheat, eggs, ricotta and candied fruit is transformed into a declaration of lust for life. Fireworks, confidences and Puccini in the kitchen.

Preparation time: 25 minutes plus soaking and chilling

Cooking time: 1¼ hours

Makes 1 x 23-cm (9-inch) cake

20g (¾oz) unsalted butter, plus extra for greasing

30g (1oz) raisins

50ml (2fl oz) milk

200g (7oz) canned cooked wheat (available in good Italian delicatessens or online)

rind of 1 lemon, cut into chunks

350g (12oz) ricotta cheese

300g (10½oz) caster sugar

3 eggs, separated

2 tablespoons orange blossom water

1 teaspoon cinnamon powder

50g (1¾oz) candied orange peel, chopped

50g (1¾oz) chopped walnuts

Pastry:

1 egg

250g (9oz) strong white flour, plus extra for dusting

100g (3½oz) caster sugar

1 teaspoon baking powder

80g (3oz) unsalted butter

30ml (1fl oz) limoncello liqueur

zest of 1 lemon

Grease and line a 23-cm (9-inch) non-stick springform cake tin with baking paper.

Place the raisins in a small bowl of water and leave to soak for 30 minutes, then drain and squeeze them dry with your hands.

Meanwhile, make the pastry. Put the egg, flour, sugar, baking powder, butter, liqueur and lemon zest into a food processor and mix together to form a dough. Roll into a ball, wrap in clingfilm and leave to rest in the refrigerator for 30 minutes.

Preheat the oven to 190°C (375°F), Gas Mark 5.

Melt the butter in a saucepan. Add the milk, wheat and lemon rind pieces and let simmer over a low heat for 10 minutes.

Beat the ricotta together with half the sugar in a bowl. In a second bowl, whisk the egg yolks with the remaining sugar until fluffy. In a third bowl, beat the egg whites together with the orange blossom water and cinnamon until stiff. Using a wooden spoon, gently mix the ingredients from all three bowls together and fold in the candied orange peel, raisins and walnut pieces.

Unwrap the chilled pastry and cut off two-thirds. Sandwich the larger piece between two sheets of baking paper and roll it out into a 29-cm (11½-inch) circle. Transfer to the base of the prepared cake tin, carefully pushing the pastry 3cm (1¼ inches) up the sides of the tin. Chill in the refrigerator for 10 minutes.

Roll out the remaining pastry between sheets of baking paper as before and cut it into 10 strips measuring 23 x 2cm (9 x ¾ inches). Arrange the strips on a sheet of lightly floured greaseproof paper and let chill in the refrigerator for 5 minutes.

Remove the base from the refrigerator and pour over the wheat cream. Gently place the pastry strips on top in a criss-cross lattice pattern and bake for 1 hour, until the strips are slightly browned and a toothpick inserted into the centre of the cake comes out clean. Leave to cool for at least 30 minutes to allow the filling to become firm before serving.

Chapter 3

LUNCH ON THE RUN

When it comes to matters of the stomach, there's no such thing as respecting the queue in Italy. On any weekday, in an *alimentari* (deli) or a *rosticceria* (rotisserie) tucked away on a side street, you will see hungry men and women, young and old, builders and bankers, pushing in front of each other with no apologies: it's lunchtime warfare. The staff at the *alimentari* will make succulent panini from scratch for customers coming in for a quick lunch between midday and 3pm (yes, that's the length of a typical lunch break in Italy, often followed by a totally deserved siesta. Of course). Usually a long queue forms behind the old lady who has unwittingly managed to get to the *alimentari* just a few minutes before everybody else. She's in no rush and takes her time choosing between a filling of Taleggio or robiola cheese, explaining to the man behind the counter why one is better than the other for her cholesterol, while remarking on the ignorance of her useless GP, who keeps telling her otherwise. But what does he know? At this point the builder impatiently waiting his turn will probably holler a typical Roman hyperbole: *'A nonna, qua stamo a fa' notte'* – 'Hey, grandma, it's getting dark outside!' This is the cue for everyone else in the shop to breathe a loud sigh of relief while nodding vigorously at each other.

And then there's the shop assistant who always slices the cured ham too thickly. He will put it on the scales and feigning innocence ask: 'It's actually 120 grams – what shall I do, shall we keep it?' No use reminding him that you had only asked for 80 grams. By this point, the customer will have been waiting in the queue for over 15 minutes and is in a hurry, having left his car parked illegally. Chances are you will later see him gesticulating wildly, trying to convince a policeman not to fine him by explaining how he absolutely had no choice but to park in front of two other vehicles on a zebra crossing. Talking loudly is considered a sign of affection in Rome. Enjoy these discussions that can stop the traffic of an entire city, where everybody is entitled to their opinion and to make it known. And all that noise only to see, five minutes later, friends and foes bite into a Rosetta con Mortazza (*see* page 69) in total #foodhappiness mood. Go hard or go home.

DIAVOLETTI
PICCANTI
CON OLIVE
DI CASTELVETRANO

e la barca va...

Pomodori ripieni con patate

RICE-STUFFED TOMATOES WITH POTATOES

This is Roman street food *par excellence*, the sort of thing you would get in a *rosticceria* to take back home or to the office. I like to inject a bit of fun into the kitchen by taking what was once in vogue and bringing it up to date, and this retro dish is definitely ready for a comeback. I love the way such simple ingredients can turn into something so tasty. Eye-catching red parcels, perfect for a cosy meal in that most exclusive restaurant: your own kitchen.

Preparation time: 30 minutes plus cooling

Cooking time: 2½ hours

Serves 6

2 tablespoons extra virgin olive oil, plus extra for oiling

2.5kg (5lb 8oz) King Edward potatoes, peeled, parboiled in salted water and cut into chunks

handful of rosemary leaves

3 garlic cloves, peeled and left whole

300ml (½ pint) vegetable stock (*see* page 12)

6 large vine tomatoes, each weighing about 200g (7oz)

2 tablespoons chopped flat-leaf parsley leaves

2 tablespoons chopped basil leaves

2 tablespoons chopped thyme leaves

180g (6oz) arborio or carnaroli risotto rice

40g (1½oz) Parmesan cheese, grated

20g (¾oz) pecorino romano cheese, grated

60g (2¼oz) scamorza, haloumi or *mozzarella da cucina* (cooking mozzarella), cut into 6 pieces

salt and pepper

Preheat the oven to 180°C (350°F), Gas Mark 4. Line two baking sheets with baking paper.

Lightly oil a Pyrex baking dish and add the parboiled potato chunks, rosemary and two garlic cloves. Cover with the stock, transfer to the oven and cook for 1 hour, or until the potatoes are soft and slightly browned at the edges. Drain the potatoes and set aside to cool.

Meanwhile, prepare the tomatoes. Slice off the top third of each tomato and reserve (these will act as the 'lids' for the stuffed tomatoes). With a spoon, scoop out the pulp and juices of the tomatoes, transfer them to a food processor and blend together until smooth. Sprinkle the inside of the tomatoes with salt and place them upside down on a wire rack to drain.

Gently fry the remaining garlic clove in the olive oil until browned, then add the blended tomato and leave to simmer for 10 minutes over a low heat until thickened. Remove the garlic, season to taste and stir in the chopped herbs. Set aside.

Boil the rice in abundant salted water according to the packet instructions until al dente, about 15–18 minutes, then drain and transfer to a bowl with the tomato sauce, grated Parmesan and pecorino. Stir together well.

Place the tomatoes on one of the prepared sheets. Fill each with a tablespoon of the rice mixture, add a piece of scamorza and cover with more rice to fill. Lay the tomato caps on the other baking sheet. Drizzle the tomatoes and lids with oil and season with pepper. Transfer to the oven, placing the tomato lids on the bottom shelf, and bake for 55 minutes, turning the grill up to high for the final 5 minutes of cooking, until golden brown.

Remove the tomatoes and lids from the oven and leave to cool for 5 minutes. Put the lids on the tomatoes and serve with the potatoes.

Rosetta con mortazza, stracchino e mostarda casalinga

ROSETTA LOAF WITH MORTADELLA, STRACCHINO CHEESE & HOMEMADE MOSTARDA

When I sneaked into the oldest *forno* in town for an impromptu lecture on Ancient Roman bread-making, the baker was surprised by my interest in this loaf. 'Rosetta is only for the sentimental retired people, who, to tell you the truth, still make the best panini with it. But it's not fashionable any more. What are you, a gladiator?' A gladiator, me? I'm just acting on common sense: try this soft, airy piece of ecstasy with mortadella, mild, creamy stracchino cheese and homemade *mostarda* and, before you know it, you'll embrace its timeless charm. Good bread calls for a golden rule: always add salt away from yeast, otherwise your attempt will be doomed from the start. But if you pay attention to a few details, the result will be so scrumptious, therapeutic and rewarding I assure you you'll want to make it a regular habit.

Preparation time: 35 minutes plus rising and cooling

Cooking time: 1¼ hours

Makes 6 sandwiches

300ml (½ pint) water

2 teaspoons fast-action dried yeast

500g (1lb 2oz) strong white flour, plus extra for dusting

50ml (2fl oz) extra virgin olive oil

1 teaspoon caster sugar

20g (¾oz) sea salt flakes

300g (10½oz) mortadella or ham of your choice

250g (9oz) stracchino or other soft cheese, cut into 6 thick slices

Mostarda (makes enough to fill 2 x 250ml/9fl oz jars):

500ml (18fl oz) water

400g (14oz) caster sugar

700g (1lb 9oz) Bramley or other cooking apples, peeled, cored and cut into wedges

130ml (4½fl oz) white wine vinegar

3 teaspoons English or wholegrain mustard

For the *mostarda*, bring the measured water to a boil in a saucepan. Stir in the sugar until fully dissolved, then add the apples and cook over a low heat for 35–40 minutes, without stirring, until the mixture is sticky and jam-like in consistency. Leave to cool for 30 minutes.

Meanwhile, heat the vinegar in another saucepan over a low heat until it is just about to boil. Stir in the mustard, transfer to a small bowl and leave to cool for 30 minutes.

Once the apple and vinegar mixtures are cool, fish the apple wedges out of their syrup and set them aside. Add the syrup to the mustardy vinegar and mix well. Pack the apple wedges into two 250-ml (9-oz) warm sterilized jars (*see* page 254), cover them with the syrup mixture, seal tightly and set aside until needed.

Line a baking tray with baking paper and fill a spray bottle with water.

Pour the measured water into a small bowl, add the yeast and stir to dissolve. Sift the flour, yeast mix and oil into a large mixing bowl or the bowl of a stand mixer with the dough hook attachment added and knead together for 10 minutes to form a dough, then add the sugar and knead for another 5 minutes. Knead for a final 5 minutes, gradually adding the salt as you go, until the dough is soft and smooth. Transfer the dough to a bowl, cover it with a clean tea towel and leave to rise in a warm place for 1½ hours.

Separate the dough into six equal-sized pieces and roll each into a ball. Place the dough balls on the lined baking tray, leaving 2cm (¾ inch) between each one.

Dust with a little flour, then, using an apple cutter, gently press down on each dough piece to about halfway in order to give the rolls their distinctive 'rosetta' markings. (If you don't have an apple cutter you can use the rim of a coffee mug to make this mark, although it won't give the bread the same distinctive shape). Cover the tray with a tea towel and leave to prove for a further 45 minutes.

Preheat the oven to 220°C (425°F), Gas Mark 7.

When you're ready to bake, dust the proved rolls with a little more flour. Spray the inside of the oven 7–8 times with your water bottle, then quickly insert the proved roll tray and close. Bake for 25–30 minutes, spraying the inside of the oven every 5 minutes, until the bread is risen and thoroughly cooked and the crust is a deep golden brown. Remove from the oven and leave to cool on a wire rack.

Cut the rosetta rolls in two horizontally, leaving the pretty rose shape intact. Divide the stracchino and mortadella evenly between the roll bottoms, spoon a little of the *mostarda* over each and sandwich together with the roll tops to close. Enjoy!

Consume your rosetta within 24 hours, or freeze it to make a stupendous packed lunch in the future. The *mostarda* will keep for up to 6 months, stored in a dry place away from sunlight.

‘Panino’ di mozzarella

MOZZARELLA ‘SANDWICH’

Wherever I may be, when the clock strikes noon, I can feel an almost tangible excitement in the air. So here is what I do: I pour myself a drink, whatever is in the house – usually the wine left over from the previous night – and set out to make some soul-satisfying food. Most of the time, it's little nibbles made with leftovers – that's when those ingredients sitting in the refrigerator looking all gloomy and disoriented come back to life and feel useful at last! This version of a mozzarella panini will transport you directly to a state of happy helplessness.

Preparation time: 10 minutes

Cooking time: 10 minutes

Serves 4

1 garlic clove, peeled and left whole

1 tablespoon extra virgin olive oil, plus extra for drizzling

1/2 courgette, thinly sliced

4 x 125-g (4½-oz) buffalo mozzarella balls, drained

1 large tomato, cut into 4 slices

small handful of basil leaves

salt and pepper

In a frying pan, heat the whole garlic clove in the oil over a medium heat for 2–3 minutes until golden. Remove and discard the garlic clove, add the courgette to the pan and cook, stirring, for 10 minutes until the courgette is soft and lightly browned. Season with salt and transfer to a small bowl.

Cut each mozzarella ball in half. Divide the courgette and tomato slices between the mozzarella halves, drizzle with oil and press the halves back together, tucking a basil leaf into each mozzarella ‘sandwich’. Season with salt and pepper to taste.

Conchiglioni ripieni su foglie di basilico

STUFFED CONCHIGLIONI PASTA ON BASIL LEAVES

On weekends, Via del Corso is where young people go to check each other out: they call it *lo struscio*, a casual stroll through the streets of the city, arms wrapped around one another companionably. In this dish, which can be enjoyed either warm or cold, the pasta shells, filled with sauce, evoke memories of this traditional Italian way of spending leisure time. Enjoy the enticing voluptuousness of making the sauce – you can take your time. Any leftover sauce makes a magnificent sandwich filling.

Preparation time: 15 minutes

Cooking time: 15 minutes

Serves 4 as a main

5 baby plum tomatoes

1 avocado

1 tablespoon salted capers, rinsed

6 tablespoons extra virgin olive oil

3 anchovy fillets in olive oil

350g (12oz) tinned tuna in spring water, drained

100g (3½oz) pitted black olives, very finely chopped

1 celery stick, trimmed and very finely chopped

1 red onion, very finely chopped

large handful of basil leaves, chopped, plus extra whole leaves to garnish

2 small handfuls of sage leaves, chopped

400g (14oz) conchiglioni pasta

1 garlic clove, peeled and left whole

large handful of flat-leaf parsley leaves

2 tablespoons breadcrumbs (*see* page 262)

1 tablespoon dried oregano

salt and white pepper

Place the tomatoes in a bowl and pour over boiling water to cover. Leave for 1–2 minutes, then drain, cut a cross at the stem end of each tomato, and peel off the skins. Cut into 5-mm (¼-inch) cubes.

Halve the avocado, scoop out the flesh with a spoon and cut into 5-mm (¼-inch) cubes. Finely chop half the capers.

Heat 1 tablespoon of olive oil together with the anchovy fillets in a large pan over a medium heat. Add the tuna, breaking up any large chunks into smaller pieces, and cook, stirring, for 5 minutes. Then stir in the tomato, avocado, chopped capers, olives, celery, onion, basil, sage and 3 tablespoons of olive oil. Season with a pinch of white pepper and remove from the heat.

Bring a large saucepan of salted water to a boil, add the conchiglioni and cook according to the packet instructions until al dente. Drain the pasta and pass it quickly under cold water to prevent it cooking further.

In a large pan, gently brown the garlic with the remaining 2 tablespoons of oil. Remove the garlic from the pan, then add the conchiglioni and mix together well, coating the pasta shells with the garlic-scented oil.

Spoon the filling into the conchiglioni. Serve in a large dish on a bed of basil leaves, scattering over the chopped parsley, breadcrumbs, oregano and the remaining whole capers to finish.

Fagottini di verza ripieni

SAVOY CABBAGE VEAL BUNDLES

This recipe is a requiem to a way of life that's now fading away. Exploding with colours, it's an inviting combination of flavours competing for your palate's attention. These tantalizing small cabbage parcels can be served warm or cold – any leftovers can be kept in the refrigerator for up to five days – and are good with a simple green salad, drizzled with balsamic vinegar. Put a considerable portion of these small cabbage parcels in an airtight container and take them to work with you for a tantalizing, flavour-filled lunch.

Preparation time: 20 minutes

Cooking time: 40 minutes

Serves 4

150g (5½oz) white cabbage, red cabbage, or chard leaves

300g (10½oz) organic minced veal (tenderloin or topside)

100g (3½oz) mortadella

50g (1¾oz) peanuts, roasted or unsalted

1 teaspoon chopped dill fronds

1 large egg

30g (1oz) Parmesan cheese, grated

1 teaspoon chopped flat-leaf parsley leaves

1 teaspoon chopped basil leaves

30g (1oz) unsalted butter

1 small white onion, chopped

50g (1¾oz) pancetta or smoked bacon cubes

1 garlic clove, peeled and left whole

2 sage leaves

50ml (2fl oz) dry white wine

120ml (4fl oz) vegetable stock

salt and pepper

Bring a large saucepan of salted water to a boil, add the cabbage leaves and blanch for 5 minutes. Drain and leave to cool on a clean tea towel.

Once the cabbage is cool, roughly chop a handful of the leaves. Put the chopped leaves into a food processor with the veal, mortadella, peanuts, dill, egg, Parmesan, parsley and basil and blend together to form a coarse paste. Season with salt and pepper.

Take a spoonful or so of the filling and place in the centre of a blanched cabbage leaf. Carefully roll the leaf up and secure it with a toothpick. Repeat with the remaining leaves and filling.

Melt the butter in a frying pan over a medium heat, add the chopped onion, bacon, garlic and sage and cook for 10 minutes until the onion has softened. Arrange the cabbage rolls in the pan, pour over the white wine and stock, season with salt and cook for 25 minutes, until the liquid has reduced to a thick, glossy sauce.

Carpaccio di spigola con pesche, kiwi e rughetta

SEA BASS CARPACCIO WITH PEACHES, KIWI & ROCKET

Carpaccio is the most sublime expression of meat or fish. Beware though, for that marvel to happen the main ingredient must be at its freshest. The most important steps of this recipe should be completed by your trusted and scrupulous fishmonger, who will fillet your sea bass, skin it and then cut it diagonally into very thin slices. From there on, it's easy peasy stuff. A riotous rainbow of colour and pattern that will brighten up even the darkest of days.

Preparation time: 10 minutes plus marinating

Serves 4

1 fennel bulb, leaves reserved to garnish

125ml (4fl oz) freshly squeezed lemon juice

50ml (2fl oz) extra virgin olive oil

pinch of sea salt flakes

1 x 600-g (1-lb 5-oz) sea bass, trimmed, filleted and cut into 50-g (1¾-oz) slices (ask your fishmonger to do this for you)

To garnish:

50g (1¾oz) wild rocket leaves

1 ripe white peach, peeled and cut into thin wedges

1 ripe kiwifruit, peeled and cut into thin slices

2 teaspoons pink peppercorns

Cut the fennel bulb into 6 slices and put into a food processor with the lemon juice, olive oil and salt. Blend everything together to form a smooth paste.

Cut each fish slice into 5 x 2.5cm (2 x 1 inch) strips. Arrange the fish pieces in the centre of a shallow serving bowl. Strain over the fennel and lemon juice mix and cover with clingfilm. Chill in the refrigerator for 30 minutes to marinate.

Once the fish has marinated, remove it from the refrigerator and garnish with the rocket, fennel leaves, fruit pieces and peppercorns. Serve immediately.

Frittata di spaghetti

SPAGHETTI OMELETTE

'Qui n'se butta gniente.' That's Roman for: 'Nothing gets thrown away here.' In the old days, lunchtime was marked by placing a huge bowl of *spaghetti al sugo* in the middle of the table, to be eaten greedily by all diners. Any leftovers would be revived in a new shape: the frittata. I must admit, I am so evangelical about the food I like eating (and cooking) that I relish an opportunity to use up ingredients that might otherwise go in the bin. The quintessential comfort food snack, *frittata di spaghetti* can also be sandwiched between pieces of bread (try the Rosetta on page 69) for a picnic: the *panino con la frittata* has been a Roman favourite for decades.

Preparation time: 10 minutes

Cooking time: 30 minutes

Serves 6

6 large eggs

50g (1¾oz) pecorino romano cheese, grated

100ml (3½fl oz) full-fat or semi-skimmed milk

pinch of salt

pinch of pepper

100g (3½oz) provolone, Muenster or mozzarella cheese, cut into 5-mm (1¼-inch) cubes

400g (14oz) spaghetti

80g (3oz) pancetta or smoked bacon cubes

6 tablespoons extra virgin olive oil

large handful of sage leaves, finely chopped, plus 10 whole sage leaves

Beat the eggs together in a bowl, add the pecorino, milk, salt, pepper and half the provolone and mix together well. Set aside.

Bring a large saucepan of salted water to a boil, add the spaghetti and cook according to the packet instructions until al dente. Drain the pasta and let it cool for a minute, then tip it back into the pan, add the beaten egg mixture and mix everything together so the pasta is evenly coated.

Heat a small non-stick frying pan over a low heat, add the pancetta and fry for 3 minutes until crisp and golden. (You won't need any oil here – the fat from the pancetta will be sufficient.) Remove the pancetta from the frying pan and set aside. Fry the whole sage leaves in the remaining pancetta fat until crispy – about 30 seconds – and set aside.

In a large non-stick frying pan, heat 4 tablespoons of the extra virgin olive oil over a medium heat. Add half the spaghetti to cover the base of the pan, scatter over the chopped sage, pancetta cubes and remaining provolone and cover with the rest of the spaghetti. Lower the heat and cook gently for 10 minutes, or until the omelette has just set. Turn the omelette over with the aid of a plate if you need it, add the remaining 2 tablespoons of olive oil and continue to cook for a further 5 minutes until the omelette is firmly set and golden in parts.

Leave the omelette to rest in the pan for 10 minutes before turning out and serving, scattered with the fried sage leaves.

Soppressata di polpo con insalata di patate e sedano

OCTOPUS 'KEBAB' WITH POTATO & CELERY SALAD

Fishermen used to beat the octopus they'd just caught against a rock to tenderize it, but I suggest you get your fishmonger to do the hard work for you. Freezing your octopus following the method outlined here will also help kickstart the tenderizing process. Once ready, you can slice the octopus thinly to serve it as a carpaccio or turn it into a lunch on the run by cutting it into thicker slices and using it to fill a panini. Octopus rules.

Preparation time: 30 minutes plus cooling and freezing

Cooking time: 1 hour 20 minutes

Serves 6

1 small carrot

1 celery stick, trimmed

1 white onion

1 tomato

2 bay leaves

1 teaspoon white vinegar

10 black peppercorns

3 juniper berries

4 cloves

100g (3½oz) coarse rock salt

1.5kg (3lb 5oz) fresh octopus, eyes and beak removed (ask your fishmonger to do this for you)

2 large Charlotte or other waxy potatoes, peeled

handful of flat-leaf parsley leaves, finely chopped

handful of dill fronds, finely chopped

1 teaspoon ground nutmeg

2 tablespoons extra virgin olive oil

Dressing:

2 tablespoons extra virgin olive oil

1 teaspoon salt

1 tablespoon pepper

4 tablespoons lemon juice

Fill a large saucepan with water, add the carrot, celery, onion, tomato, bay leaves, vinegar, peppercorns, juniper berries, cloves and salt and bring to a boil.

Carefully lower the octopus briefly into the water until fully submerged, then lift it out of the pan. Repeat this process 9 more times, until the tentacles have curled up and softened, then lower the octopus once more into the water. Cover with a lid, and leave to simmer gently over a very low heat for 50 minutes, then add the potatoes and cook for a further 30 minutes.

Once the cooking time is up, remove the vegetables from the cooking liquid. Finely slice the celery and dice the potatoes into 1-cm (½-inch) cubes, put in a bowl and leave to chill in the refrigerator. Leave the octopus to cool in its cooking liquid for 30 minutes (this will prevent it from getting chewy), then drain and pat dry with kitchen paper. Cut the octopus into six big chunks, leaving the tentacles intact.

With a sharp knife, cut off the tapered end of an empty 1.5-litre (2½-pint) plastic bottle and pierce the bottom with a pair of scissors or the tip of a sharp knife. Resting the bottle in the sink, insert the octopus and let the excess water drain through the holes you've made at the bottom of the bottle. Using something heavy like a meat tenderizer or a pestle, push the octopus as far down into the bottle as it can go, then cover with clingflim and place a can of beans or tomatoes on top to act as a weight. Transfer to the freezer and leave for at least 10 hours.

When ready to serve, remove the octopus bottle from the freezer, turn the bottle upside down and let the octopus slide out. Using a sharp knife, cut the octopus 'kebab' into either thin or thick slices, according to your taste.

For the dressing, mix together the ingredients in a small bowl until well combined. Drizzle over the octopus slices.

Arrange the potatoes and celery in a serving dish and top with the dressed octopus slices. Scatter over the parsley and dill, sprinkle over the nutmeg and drizzle with olive oil.

MELANZANE E ZUCCHINE A BARCHETTA
AUBERGINE & COURGETTE 'BOATS'

This recipe, with its elaborate simplicity, is like a witty conversation that touches the heart with exquisite common sense and deadpan humour but doesn't take long to get to the point with a matter-of-fact flair. An enticing, all-year-round vegetable dish.

Preparation time: 20 minutes, plus resting

Cooking time: 1 hour 20 minutes

Serves 4 as a main

Aubergine 'boats':

2 large aubergines (about 350g/12oz each), trimmed and cut in half

1 tablespoon extra virgin olive oil, plus extra for oiling

4 salted anchovies, rinsed and chopped

60g (2¼oz) pitted black olives, chopped

1 teaspoon chopped flat-leaf parsley leaves

80g (3oz) breadcrumbs (*see* page 262)

1 garlic clove, sliced

1 teaspoon dried oregano

50g (1¾oz) salted capers, rinsed

100g (3½oz) cherry tomatoes, halved

salt and pepper

Courgette 'boats':

4 large courgettes

200g (7oz) roast ham, finely chopped

150g (5½oz) provolone or scamorza cheese, finely chopped

1 teaspoon ground nutmeg

pinch of chilli flakes

1 tablespoon extra virgin olive oil

150g (5½oz) strong Cheddar cheese

For the aubergine 'boats', score the flesh of each aubergine half with a sharp knife in a criss-cross pattern, sprinkle with 2 tablespoons of salt and leave to rest skin-side down on a wire rack for 1 hour to extract any bitter juices. Rinse and dry the aubergine halves with kitchen paper or a clean tea towel.

Preheat the oven to 170°C (340°F), Gas Mark 3. Lightly oil two baking dishes.

Mix the chopped anchovies, olives and parsley together in a bowl. Add the breadcrumbs and stir in the garlic, oregano and capers. Season with salt and pepper and mix together well.

Arrange the aubergine halves in one of the prepared baking dishes, divide the tomato halves equally between them and spoon over the breadcrumb mixture. Drizzle over the oil and bake in the oven for 1 hour until the breadcrumb mix is golden and the aubergines are soft and tender. Remove from the oven and set aside.

For the courgette 'boats', bring a large saucepan of salted water to a boil. Add the whole courgettes and boil for 5 minutes, then drain and leave to cool.

Increase the heat to 200°C (400°F), Gas Mark 6.

When the courgettes are cool enough to handle, trim the ends and cut in half. Using a spoon, gently scoop the softer flesh from the middle, strain it to remove any excess water and put it in a bowl along with the chopped ham, provolone, nutmeg, chilli flakes and olive oil. Season with salt and mix everything together well.

Spoon the stuffing into the hollowed out courgette halves and place them in the second prepared baking dish. Top each 'boat' with a fine grating of Cheddar cheese and bake in the oven for 10 minutes until the cheese has melted and the filling is golden. Serve alongside the courgettes either warm or cold, accompanied by an equally healthy green salad.

Gnocchi alla ricotta del giovedì con gamberetti e pistacchi

THURSDAY'S RICOTTA GNOCCHI WITH PRAWNS & PISTACHIOS

A few years ago, I realized that my job as a journalist didn't allow me to do justice to all the tiny details of life that fascinated me. That was when I started to live and breathe through the redemptive power of food. Just like my career path, preparing gnocchi is a slow-building process. Historically, it made sense for Catholics to eat something filling on Thursday, the day before they were forbidden to eat meat. *Ridi, ridi, che mamma ha fatto i gnocchi.* Keep smiling, all is well, mummy made you gnocchi.

Preparation time: 30 minutes plus cooling

Cooking time: 25 minutes

Serves 6

1.5kg (3lb 5oz) Maris Piper or other floury potatoes, peeled and cut into 1-cm (1/2-inch) chunks

450g (1lb) plain flour, plus extra for dusting

100g (31/2oz) ricotta cheese

1 large egg

salt

Sauce:

4 tablespoons extra virgin olive oil

1 garlic clove, peeled and left whole

500g (1lb 2oz) cooked peeled king prawns

150g (51/2oz) unsalted pistachios, crushed to a fine powder

40g (11/2oz) unsalted butter, cut into 1-cm 1/2-inch cubes

Bring a large saucepan of salted water to a boil, add the potato chunks and cook over a medium heat for 10–15 minutes, until the potato pieces are completely cooked through but not so soft that they are falling apart. Drain and set aside until cool enough to handle, then mash them with a potato masher or fork until smooth. Season with salt to taste and set aside to cool.

For the sauce, heat the oil in a large frying pan over a low heat, add the garlic clove and cook gently until golden to infuse its flavour into the hot oil. Remove the garlic, add the prawns to the pan along with half the crushed pistachios and cook for 5 minutes until the prawns are just lightly golden but not overcooked. Remove the pan from the heat, add the butter and stir to melt into the hot prawns. Set aside.

In a large bowl, mix the flour, ricotta and egg together with the mashed potato mixture using your hands until everything comes together to form a soft, yellow dough. Tip the dough out onto a lightly floured work surface and knead for 2–3 minutes until firm, then divide into quarters. Roll each piece of dough into a cylinder roughly 3cm (11/4 inches) thick and divide each into 2-cm (3/4-inch) pieces. Lightly press down on each gnocchi with the tines of a fork to give them their typical curly shape and dust with a little more flour.

Bring a large saucepan of salted water to a boil. Place a serving bowl by the side of the hob and fill it with half the sauce along with a ladleful of the boiling salted water.

Add the gnocchi to the pan and poach for 2–3 minutes, or until they float up to the surface of the water. As the gnocchi come to the surface, scoop them up with a slotted spoon and place them in the bowl with the sauce. Spoon over the remaining sauce and fold gently to mix well, then sprinkle over the rest of the pistachios to finish. Serve outrageously hot.

Ceci e baccalà

FRIDAY'S SALT COD WITH CHICKPEAS

Some like it hot. I like it not. This dish is divine served cold on the day of the week when Romans traditionally renounce meat to offer patronage to the best fish in town. When preparing this dish, I go for convenience. Italian cooking is not that complicated, really. It just takes time. For this recipe, you would usually use salt cod, which needs to be soaked for about 24 hours, but I'd rather go with the fresh version, which is less salty and more tender. The cooking method is *al guazzetto*, that is to say, in a very fluid wine sauce.

Preparation time: 10 minutes

Cooking time: 15-20 minutes

Serves 4

150ml (5fl oz) vegetable stock

6 tablespoons extra virgin olive oil

1 garlic clove, peeled and left whole

2 rosemary sprigs, leaves picked

1 teaspoon ground cumin

handful of sage leaves

2 x 250-g (9-oz) cans cooked
   chickpeas in water, drained

600g (1lb 5oz) cod, haddock or
   monkfish fillets

50g (1¾oz) plain flour

1 teaspoon salt

large handful of kaffir lime leaves

100ml (3½fl oz) dry white wine

Gently warm the stock in a saucepan.

Heat half the oil in a frying pan over a medium heat. Add the garlic clove, rosemary leaves, cumin and sage leaves and fry gently for 2–3 minutes until the garlic is browned. Remove and discard the garlic, add the chickpeas, season with salt and cook for 5–10 minutes, until the chickpeas have softened and are beginning to break up. Pour the contents of the pan into a food processor and blend together, gradually adding the warm stock, until purée-like in consistency. Return to the pan and keep warm.

Drain and rinse the fish well, then cut it into 1-cm (½-inch) cubes. Put the flour and salt in a bowl, add the fish cubes and toss to coat evenly.

Heat the remaining oil in a large frying pan. Wrap each fish cube in a lime leaf, securing it in place with a toothpick. Transfer the mini fish parcels to the pan and cook for 1 minute on each side, then add the wine and bring to a vigorous simmer. Cook for 5 minutes until the wine has evaporated, then remove from the heat and serve with the chickpea purée.

Chapter 4 FAMILY LUNCHES

On Sundays, the world stops in Rome. The streets fall quiet at lunchtime. The busiest places around midday are either churches or *pasticcerie*, where Romans buy *pastarelle* (*see* page 30) for their families – having been instructed not to dare come home empty-handed – while inside the houses, everyone's attention is focused on the kitchen. The youngest child is often entrusted with the fundamental task of verifying that the pasta is cooked al dente, while the older kids set the table. Over lunch, the mother will gently (or not so gently) slap the arms of the little ones to remind them of their table manners – 'Don't slouch!', 'Get your elbows off the table!' – while the nonno will make a toast to celebrate the day of rest, with his glass filled half with red wine and half with water.

At *il pranzo della domenica*, superstitions passed down from generation to generation are still observed. For example, having 13 people around a table is considered akin to inviting bad luck. Should you accidentally find yourself with 13 for lunch, you can always have the children sit at a separate table. No children in the family? Just set an extra place with an empty chair. Spilling salt on the tablecloth or pretty much anywhere else is also inauspicious. Should that happen, you must throw a pinch of salt over your left shoulder with your right hand. Spilling wine, however, brings good luck, so much so that each diner must immediately dip a finger in the spilled wine and dab the back of their ears in order to share in the inevitable good fortune that will surely follow. These gestures are all part of a mosaic, a form of magical interpretation of reality, and the following chapter is both a walk down memory lane and a vivid look at modernity.

In order to demonstrate a respectable measure of conviviality, every Italian table will have at least one loaf of bread on it. After overindulging in Sunday's Pasticcio di Cappelletti (*see* page 114) or ornamental Vitel Tonné (*see* page 118), most of us opt for a *scarpetta*: we take a piece of bread and mop up the delicious leftover sauce on our plate. It'd be bad manners and bad luck not to. Beware of all imitations.

Gnocchi alla Romana con sugo di spuntature di maiale

ROMAN-STYLE SEMOLINA GNOCCHI WITH PORK RIB SAUCE

In Ancient Rome people didn't believe that creativity came from human beings. They gave credit to a heavenly spirit that came from some otherworldly place: *il Genio*. This spirit would subtly reveal itself to the artist, guiding him or her. My beloved readers, just like those artists I need divine intervention to protect myself from over-testing this recipe. Not an easy task, as these pork ribs are a delectably juicy pleasure, which could very well be out of this world.

Preparation time: 30 minutes plus cooling

Cooking time: 2½ hours

Serves 6

1 litre (1¾ pints) milk

100g (3½oz) unsalted butter, plus extra for greasing

2 teaspoons ground nutmeg

2 juniper berries, crushed

250g (9oz) semolina

2 egg yolks, beaten

150g (5½oz) Parmesan cheese, grated

salt

Sauce:

80ml (3fl oz) extra virgin olive oil

1 large white onion, roughly chopped

1 celery stick, trimmed and roughly chopped

1 carrot, roughly chopped

600g (1lb 5oz) pork ribs

600g (1lb 5oz) pork sausages

1kg (2lb 4oz) passata (sieved tomatoes)

2 cloves

handful of thyme leaves, chopped

pinch of chilli flakes (optional)

salt

For the sauce, heat the oil in a large saucepan over a low heat, add the onion, celery and carrot and cook gently, stirring occasionally, for 15 minutes, until softened and golden.

Remove the vegetables from the pan and set aside. Add the pork ribs and sausages and brown well on all sides, then pour over the passata and 100ml (3½fl oz) of water. Return the vegetables to the pan, bring to a gentle simmer and cook over a low heat, covered, for 1 hour. Season with salt, stir in the cloves, thyme and chilli flakes, if using, and cook for a further 1 hour, until the sauce has thickened and reduced. Remove from the heat and set aside.

For the semolina gnocchi, heat the milk together with a knob of butter, the nutmeg, juniper berries and a generous pinch of salt in a large saucepan. Bring to a boil, then gradually sift in the semolina, stirring vigorously with a whisk to prevent any lumps from forming. Cook over low heat for 3 minutes, until the semolina is thick enough for a spoon to stand up in the mixture, then remove the pan from the heat and leave to cool slightly for 10 minutes.

Preheat the oven to 180°C (350°F), Gas Mark 4. Grease one 33 x 23-cm (13 x 9-inch) baking dish and a second 23 x 23-cm (9 x 9-inch) baking dish with a little butter.

Once the semolina mixture has cooled, stir in the egg yolks and half the grated Parmesan. Pour the mixture into the large prepared baking dish to a layer of about 1cm (½ inch). Wet your hands and press your palms on the semolina to level it off. Leave to cool for a further 15 minutes.

Using the rim of a wine glass, cut out as many discs as the amount of semolina allows. Arrange the discs in the regular baking dish, overlapping them slightly, and sprinkle with the remaining Parmesan. Melt the remaining butter and drizzle over the semolina gnocchi.

Bake the gnocchi for 25–30 minutes, until golden. Warm the tomato sauce and serve with the gnocchi.

*Coda di rospo agli agrumi e finocchio accompagnata da fagiolini corallo
in salsa di noci, melograno e mango*

CITRUSY MONKFISH WITH FENNEL ACCOMPANIED BY RUNNER BEANS IN A WALNUT, MANGO & POMEGRANATE DRESSING

With its bright citrus flavours, this is honest, straightforward, uplifting food. In Rome, runner beans are called *fagioli corallo* or coral beans, probably because they look as if they might grow underwater. In trattorias, you will find them floating in tomato sauce. This side dish proves that in the kitchen, as in life, there's something more important than logic: imagination.

Preparation time: 15 minutes

Cooking time: 25 minutes

Serves 6

100g (3½oz) plain flour

6 monkfish fillets, cut into 1-cm (½-inch) cubes

4 tablespoons extra virgin olive oil

50g (1¾oz) unsalted butter

2 fennel bulbs, cut into 1-cm (½-inch) chunks and fronds reserved

120ml (4fl oz) water

4 tablespoons lemon juice

2 teaspoons fennel seeds

salt and white pepper

Runner beans:

1 garlic clove, peeled and left whole

600g (1lb 5oz) runner beans, trimmed

25g (1oz) chives, finely chopped

8 walnuts, shelled

1 tablespoon grated Parmesan cheese

2 tablespoons white wine vinegar

4 tablespoons extra virgin olive oil

¼ large mango, peeled and diced

100g (3½oz) pomegranate seeds

salt and pepper

For the runner beans, half fill a large pan with water, add the garlic clove and bring to a boil. Add the runner beans to the pan with a little salt and cook for 5 minutes or until tender, then drain well under cold water, reserving 3 tablespoons of the garlicky cooking water. Set aside.

Mix the chives, walnuts, Parmesan, vinegar, olive oil, mango, pomegranate seeds and reserved cooking water together in a small bowl. Season with salt and pepper to taste and set aside.

Put the flour in a large food bag together with the monkfish pieces and shake to coat.

Gently heat the oil and butter together in a large casserole dish. Add the fennel chunks and measured water, increase the heat to medium and let simmer for 10 minutes, then stir in the coated fish pieces, lemon juice and fennel seeds. Season with salt and white pepper to taste.

Cook for a further 10 minutes, turning the fish pieces occasionally to ensure they are evenly cooked. Scatter over the fennel fronds and serve immediately with the lemon slices and alongside the beans, drizzling over the dressing before serving.

Spiedini di manzo ripieni con tortino di agretti

FILLED BEEF ROLLS WITH AGRETTI TART

In Rome, if you look closely, reminders of the past are everywhere. In a city that is already the epitome of vintage, you'll find shops selling all kinds of memorabilia, like posters for Italian neorealist films, depicting post-war Rome as if suspended in time, radiating monumental grandeur and unattainable virtues.

For me, this stupendously colourful dish – the perfect excuse to use up any odds and ends you have lurking in the refrigerator – encapsulates the sense of nostalgia that permeates the city. When shopping for this recipe, look for radicchio with crisp leaves, with no signs of wilting or browning. This dish also features agretti (also known as friar's beard), a grass-like Italian green with a delicately mineral taste, though you can use samphire instead should it prove difficult to find.

Preparation time: 15 minutes

Cooking time: 1 hour 25 minutes

Serves 6

5 tablespoons extra virgin olive oil, plus extra for brushing

2 large red onions, 1 finely sliced, 1 cut into quarters and separated into petals

150g (5½oz) chicory heads, trimmed and finely sliced

150g (5½oz) breadcrumbs (*see* page 262)

500g (1lb 2oz) beef fillet, cut into 5-mm (¼-inch) slices

150g (5½oz) prosciutto or roast ham, roughly chopped

150g (5½oz) Fontina, provolone or Bel Paese cheese, roughly chopped

24 bay leaves

Tortino di agretti:

20ml (4fl oz) extra virgin olive oil

1 small red onion, thinly sliced

200g (7oz) agretti (friar's beard) or samphire

Place six bamboo skewers in a bowl, cover them with water and leave them to soak (this will prevent them from burning later during cooking).

Heat 3 tablespoons of olive oil in a non-stick frying pan over a medium heat, add the sliced onion and cook for 5 minutes until golden. Remove and set aside half the onion, add the chicory, reduce the heat to low and cook for a further 15 minutes, until the chicory has softened and is tender.

Tip the chicory mixture into a food processor and blend together with 50g (1¾oz) of the breadcrumbs to form a smooth paste.

Using a rolling pin, flatten the beef slices on a clean work surface until they measure roughly 10cm (4 inches) in diameter. Cut each slice in two. Place a tablespoon of the chicory mixture and a teaspoon each of the chopped prosciutto and cheese in the centre of each beef piece and wrap everything up like a parcel. Repeat with the remaining beef pieces until all the ingredients are used.

Alternately thread the meat parcels, bay leaves and onion petals onto the soaked bamboo skewers, allowing four meat parcels per skewer. Brush the skewers with a little oil and coat with the remaining breadcrumbs. Set aside.

For the *tortino*, heat the oil in a non-stick frying pan over a low heat, add the onion and a pinch of salt and cook for 5 minutes, until the onion has started to soften. Increase the heat to medium, add the agretti and three-quarters of the radicchio, cover and cook for a further 10 minutes until the leaves have wilted and are soft. Remove the lid and cook for a further 1–2 minutes, then season with salt and pepper and set aside.

Preheat the oven to 180°C (350°F), Gas Mark 4. Lightly butter a 16-cm (6¼-inch) round cake tin. Alternatively, to make individual servings, lightly butter 6 ramekins or 6 holes of a muffin pan. Using the bottom of

300g (10½oz) Trevisano radicchio bulbs or red chicory heads, trimmed and cut into strips

unsalted butter, for greasing

300g (10½oz) ricotta cheese

50g (1¾oz) Parmesan cheese, grated

1 egg, plus 2 egg whites

salt and pepper

To garnish:

drizzle of balsamic vinegar

50g (1¾oz) croutons

a ramekin or muffin mould as a guide, cut out 6 circles of baking paper and place one in the bottom of each ramekin or muffin mould.

Beat the ricotta in a bowl with a wooden spoon until creamy and fluffy, then stir in the cooked vegetables, Parmesan, egg and egg whites. Season generously with salt and pepper and mix together well.

Place the cake tin on a baking tray with high sides. Pour the filling into the tin, then pour boiling water into the tray up to two-thirds of the tin's height. Carefully transfer to the oven and bake for about 45–50 minutes (or 20–25 minutes if using ramekins or a muffin pan), until the *tortino* is set and lightly golden. Remove from the oven and leave to cool.

While the *tortino* is cooling, cook the *spiedini*. Heat the remaining 2 tablespoons of olive oil in a non-stick frying pan, add the skewers and brown them gently for 3 minutes per side until shiny and golden.

Arrange the *spiedini* on a platter. Cut the *tortino* into wedges and garnish with the croutons, a drizzle of balsamic vinegar and the reserved radicchio and onion. Serve.

Pasta al forno con asparagi, pancetta e provola

BAKED PASTA WITH ASPARAGUS, PANCETTA & PROVOLA CHEESE

Meals with friends and family call for comfort food, and the addition of asparagus turns a pasta bake into a feast. This dish is just as mouth-watering when eaten cold, making a yummy treat for a refrigerator raider like me. Topped with pancetta, this dish is an overwhelming embrace of the senses. Tall or short, wise or fool, believe me, no-one can resist it.

Preparation time: 20 minutes

Cooking time: 1 hour

Serves 6

500g (1lb 2oz) asparagus or wild asparagus

30ml (1fl oz) extra virgin olive oil

1 leek, trimmed, cleaned and finely sliced

100g (3½oz) unsalted butter, plus extra for greasing

500ml (18fl oz) milk

1 teaspoon ground nutmeg

100g (3½oz) plain flour

400g (14oz) fusilli or penne pasta

150g (5½oz) provolone, Fontina or medium Cheddar cheese

150g (5½oz) pancetta or smoked bacon cubes

50g (1¾oz) breadcrumbs (*see* page 262)

salt

Prepare the asparagus by breaking off and discarding the woody ends, cutting off and reserving the tips and slicing the stalks into 1-cm (½-inch) chunks.

Put the asparagus tips into a small saucepan of boiling salted water and blanch for 3 minutes. Drain and set aside.

Bring a second saucepan of salted water to a boil, lower to a gentle simmer and keep to one side.

Heat the olive oil in a non-stick frying pan, add the leek and cook, stirring, for 5 minutes until browned. Add the asparagus stalks, season with salt and cook for 20 minutes, stirring occasionally and adding a ladleful of hot water every 5 minutes to prevent everything sticking to the bottom of the pan, until the asparagus stalks are soft and cooked through. Tip the asparagus and leek mixture into a food processor and blend together well. Set aside.

Preheat the oven to 180°C (350°F), Gas Mark 4. Grease a 35-cm (14-inch) x 20-cm (8-inch) oven dish with a little butter.

Gently heat the milk in a small saucepan, ensuring it doesn't boil. In a separate saucepan, melt the butter, add the nutmeg and flour and stir together to make a smooth paste (roux). Season with salt and slowly add the warm milk, stirring constantly, to form a smooth, creamy sauce. Bring to a gentle boil, then remove from the heat and set aside.

Bring a large saucepan of salted water to a boil, add the pasta and cook for half the cooking time indicated on the packet, or about 3–7 minutes. Drain and place in a bowl along with the sauce, two-thirds of the provolone and half the blended asparagus. Mix everything together well and pour into the prepared oven dish.

Scatter over the asparagus tips and pancetta cubes, pour over the remaining asparagus mixture and sprinkle with the remaining provolone. Transfer to the oven and bake for 20–25 minutes, or until the surface has formed a nice golden crust.

Sprinkle over the breadcrumbs and cut into rectangles. Serve hot or cold.

Filetto di salmone con mousse di fave e pecorino

SALMON FILLET
WITH BROAD BEAN & PECORINO MOUSSE

It's May 1st, also known as Workers' Day. From this date on, a string of public holidays and long weekends signal the beginning of summer and its seemingly endless sweet idleness. It's picnic time, and families will arrive in the meadows of the Castelli Romani with baskets filled with bottles of red wine, fresh broad beans and crystalline pecorino. As the popular proverb says, *'Al cuor non si comanda'* ('you can't rule the heart'). It wants what it wants. Still, how about some pink salmon with minty broad bean mousse as a variation on the theme? Sit down. Tuck that napkin in your collar. Get ready to have your taste buds driven insane.

Preparation time: 10 minutes

Cooking time: 10 minutes

Serves 2

250g (9oz) podded broad beans or edamame, defrosted if frozen

2 tablespoons lemon juice

30g (1oz) mint leaves, plus extra to garnish

50g (1¾oz) pecorino romano cheese

4 tablespoons extra virgin olive oil

knob of salted butter

2 x 260-g (9½-oz) salmon fillets

salt

Bring a saucepan of salted water to a boil, add the broad beans and cook for 5 minutes. Drain and skin the beans, then put them in a food processor with the lemon juice, mint leaves, pecorino and olive oil. Season with salt and blend together briefly for 5 seconds to form a coarsely chopped 'mousse'.

Melt a little butter in a frying pan over a low heat, add the salmon fillets and cook for 3–5 minutes on each side until lightly golden.

Transfer the salmon fillets to individual plates and spread the broad bean mousse over the surface of each. Scatter over a few extra mint leaves and enjoy with a full-flavoured white wine such as Greco di Tufo.

Pasta alla carbonara

PASTA WITH CARBONARA SAUCE

For centuries, atoning for their sins by paying for the construction and decoration of churches was the standard way of life for Roman nobility. Caravaggio got in on the act, befriending the rich families of his day, and inside the Basilica di Sant'Agostino hangs his *Madonna di Loreto.* Caravaggio used his friends as models, and his Mary is sensuous and real. He also illuminated the scene in a way that proved revolutionary. Let there be light, then.

We find the same shining light in *pasta alla carbonara,* the apotheosis of the Roman kitchen, which owes its name to the charcoal burners (*carbonari*) who used to leave for work with some handy ingredients from which to make lunch. They might have let some coal dust slip in, hence the black peppery finish.

Preparation time: 5 minutes plus chilling

Cooking time: 20 minutes

Serves 4

20 black peppercorns

5 egg yolks, plus 1 egg white

200g (7oz) pecorino romano cheese, grated

a sprinkle of ground nutmeg

200g (7oz) pancetta cubes

400g (14oz) spaghetti

salt

Toast the peppercorns in a small frying pan over a gentle heat for 1–2 minutes until fragrant, then grind or crush them to a rough powder using a pestle and mortar, a meat tenderizer or the flat side of a heavy knife.

Transfer the grated pecorino cheese to a food processor and whiz briefly – you want the pecorino to be as finely grated as possible.

In a bowl, whisk together the egg yolks and white for 2–3 minutes until pale and creamy. Add two-thirds of the pecorino and mix together well, until glossy and thick. Sprinkle over the nutmeg and a little of the crushed pepper, transfer to the refrigerator and leave to chill for 20 minutes.

Fry the pancetta in a small frying pan over a medium heat, stirring, for 10 minutes until lightly golden (you won't need any oil for this, as the pancetta will release a lot of fat while cooking). Spoon off and discard half the fat from the pan and set the pancetta and remaining fat aside.

Bring a large saucepan of salted water to a boil, add the spaghetti and cook according to the packet instructions until al dente. Drain the pasta, reserving a cupful of the cooking water, and return to the pan.

Pour the chilled egg and cheese mixture over the pasta, then add the crispy pancetta and fat. Quickly stir everything together, adding a splash or two of the reserved cooking water, until the sauce is smooth and creamy. Sprinkle over the rest of the cheese and pepper and serve immediately.

Spezzatino in umido con parmigiana di carciofi
BEEF STEW WITH ARTICHOKE PARMIGIANA

Braised in excellent olive oil, with the meat allowed to steep in its own juices until it is done, this beef stew is like a good marriage: the whole is greater than the sum of its parts. You can enjoy this *spezzatino* either *in bianco* – with white sauce, as suggested here – or *in rosso*, by adding 50g (1³/₄oz) of tomato concentrate for a red sauce. And to simply call artichoke parmigiana a side dish is to underestimate this sumptuous treat. In fact, together, these two dishes make for a perfect gastronomical marriage.

Preparation time: 10 minutes

Cooking time: 2 hours

Serves 8

80g (3oz) plain flour

1.5kg (3lb 5 oz) beef steak, cut into 5-cm (2-inch) chunks

knob of unsalted butter

70g (2¹/₂oz) pancetta cubes

1 small carrot, very finely chopeed

1 celery stick, trimmed and very finely chopped

1 shallot, very finely chopped

1 garlic clove, peeled and left whole

4 tablespoons extra virgin olive oil

150ml (¹/₄ pint) red wine

500ml (18fl oz) beef stock

2 teaspoons dried rosemary

handful of sage leaves

1 bay leaf, plus extra to garnish

salt and pepper

Artichoke parmigiana:

knob of unsalted butter

1 garlic clove, peeled and left whole

1 large white onion, very finely chopped

250ml (9fl oz) passata (sieved tomatoes)

4 tablespoons dry white wine

1 teaspoon ground nutmeg

Place the flour in a plastic food bag, add the beef pieces and shake to coat.

Melt a little butter in a large saucepan over a medium heat. Add the pancetta, carrot, celery, shallot and garlic and cook, stirring, for 5 minutes or until lightly browned. Stir in the oil and wine and cook for a further 2–3 minutes, then add the coated beef pieces. Cook, stirring, for another 2–3 minutes until the beef pieces are browned on all sides, then pour over the stock and bring to a boil. Add the rosemary, sage and bay leaf, reduce the heat to a simmer and cook, covered, for 1 hour 20 minutes. Uncover and simmer for another 30 minutes, or until the beef is tender and the sauce has thickened and reduced. (If the sauce is still quite liquid at this point, increase the heat and cook for a bit longer until it's reduced to the desired consistency). Season with salt and pepper.

While the beef is cooking, make the artichoke parmigiana. Melt the butter in a saucepan over a low heat, add the garlic and onion and cook gently, stirring occasionally, for 5 minutes until golden. Increase the heat to medium, then add the passata, wine, nutmeg, basil and mint. Simmer gently for 20–25 minutes until the sauce has thickened and reduced, season with salt and set aside.

Whisk the beer, flour and egg together in a small bowl to form a batter.

Drain the prepared artichoke quarters and cut them lengthways into 1-cm (¹/₂-inch) slices. Leave the slices to dry between tea towels.

Pour the vegetable oil into a large, heavy-based saucepan and heat it until it is almost smoking. Dip the artichoke slices in the batter, then carefully lower them into the hot oil and fry for 3 minutes until lightly golden (you may need to do this in batches so as not to overcrowd the pan). Remove the artichoke slices with a slotted spoon and drain on kitchen paper.

Preheat the oven to 180°C (350°F), Gas Mark 4.

Smear the bottom of a baking dish with 4 tablespoons of the tomato sauce. Layer the artichokes on top of the sauce, followed by a layer of the cheese slices. Scatter over a little of the grated Parmesan and some of the remaining basil and mint. Continue to layer in this manner until all the

handful of basil leaves, chopped,
plus extra to serve

handful of mint leaves, chopped,
plus extra to serve

150ml (¼ pint) beer

70g (2½oz) plain flour

1 egg

8 globe artichokes, cleaned (see
page 13), quartered lengthways
and placed in acidulated water

200ml (⅓ pint) vegetable oil

200g (7oz) provolone, scamorza,
mozzarella da cucina (cooking
mozzarella) or medium Cheddar
cheese, cut into 1-cm (½-inch)
slices

150g (5½oz) Parmesan cheese,
grated

salt

ingredients have been used up, finishing with a last layer of tomato sauce.
Bake for 30 minutes until the tomato sauce is bubbling and the surface has
slightly browned. Scatter some bay leaves on top to garnish.

Leave the parmigiana to rest for 10 minutes, then scatter with a few extra
mint and basil leaves before serving alongside the stew.

Pesce spada al cartoccio con polpo e scarola in padella

SWORDFISH EN PAPILLOTE WITH OCTOPUS & SAUTÉED LETTUCE

I really admire people who can neatly debone a fish. It definitely does not come easily to me. As the fish is carried to the table, my inner monologue begins: 'Will you be kind to me? Oh, don't be such a rascal, people are watching.' That's why I often like to cook fish *en papillote* – it is so tender that even the clumsiest eater will be won over. I like to accompany it with baby octopus (if you buy it fresh, freeze it for at least a day before using), luscious crispy morsels cooked in the oven to spare your kitchen the smell of deep-frying. As for the *scarola*, the marriage of salty capers and sweet sultanas is what makes this lettuce dish so delicious. The flavours are going to send you to the moon and back. Totally worth the journey.

Preparation time: 15 minutes

Cooking time: 30 minutes

Serves 6

60g (2¼oz) plain flour

300g (10½oz) baby octopus, cleaned and roughly chopped

6 swordfish steaks, cut into chunks

5 tablespoons extra virgin olive oil

4 tablespoons dry white wine

3 tablespoons chopped thyme leaves

salt and white pepper

Scarola in padella:

1½ tablespoons extra virgin olive oil

3 garlic cloves, peeled and left whole

50g (1¾oz) raisins

50g (1¾oz) pine nuts

8 anchovies in olive oil

50g (1¾oz) Kalamata olives, pitted

50g (1¾oz) salted capers, rinsed

1kg (2lb 4oz) scarola (prickly lettuce) or chicory, trimmed and leaves separated

Preheat the oven to 200°C (400°F), Gas Mark 6.

Put the flour and baby octopus pieces in a large food bag with a few generous pinches of salt and shake well to coat.

Season the swordfish pieces generously with salt and white pepper and brush with 2 tablespoons of the oil. Place a large rectangle of baking paper in a large oven dish and pour over the wine. Arrange the swordfish pieces in the centre of the paper and sprinkle over the thyme, then wrap the paper up to form a loose parcel.

Take a second large rectangle of baking paper and brush it with 1 tablespoon of oil. Place it next to the swordfish parcel in the oven dish and spread over the octopus pieces. Drizzle over the remaining oil.

Transfer the dish to the oven and cook for 15 minutes. Remove the swordfish parcel from the oven and leave to rest while you return the octopus to the oven and cook for a further 15 minutes until lightly golden and crispy around the edges.

Meanwhile, prepare the *scarola*. Warm the olive oil in a large non-stick frying pan over a medium heat, add the garlic cloves and cook for 3 minutes until brown. Remove the garlic from the pan and add the raisins, pine nuts, anchovies, olives and capers. Cook, stirring continuously, for 2–3 minutes until the anchovies have almost dissolved, then add the lettuce, cover the pan and leave to cook gently for 15 minutes, or until the lettuce has wilted and turned a glossy green.

Carefully unwrap the swordfish parcel and transfer the fish pieces to a serving dish. Top with the crispy octopus and serve alongside the lettuce.

Pasticcio di cappelletti panna, prosciutto, fegatini e piselli

CAPPELLETTI PASTA CAKE WITH CREAM, HAM, LIVER & PEAS

In Rome's elite gentleman's club, Circolo della Caccia, princes and marquises discuss the profitability of their lands without ever mentioning the m-word (money) over dinner. The idea of waiters handing individual plated servings to diners is unthinkable here. To bring a serving dish brimming with fragrant delights to the table signifies abundance and conviviality, and waiters gracefully distribute their gastronomic sculptures. Speaking of which, it was once a source of pride for Roman nobility to commission Bernini to chisel their main course. *Pasticcio* is a baroque dish, and I take delight in carving flowers for this luxuriant pasta cake.

Preparation time: 30 minutes plus soaking

Cooking time: 50 minutes

Serves 8 as a main

30g (1oz) dried porcini mushrooms (ceps)

4 tablespoons extra virgin olive oil

200g (7oz) leeks, trimmed, cleaned and sliced

150g (5½oz) chicken livers, trimmed and chopped

250g (9oz) frozen garden peas

150g (5½oz) roast ham, cut into 5mm (¼ inch) strips

1 teaspoon ground nutmeg

600g (1lb 5oz) prosciutto cappelletti, Bolognese tortellini or cheese and smoked ham tortellini

400ml (14fl oz) double cream

200g (7oz) Parmesan cheese, grated

unsalted butter, for greasing

2 x 320-g (11½-oz) shortcrust pastry sheets, thawed if frozen

1 large egg yolk, beaten

salt and pepper

Put the dried porcini into a small bowl and cover with 100ml (3½fl oz) of warm water. Leave to soak for 10 minutes.

Heat the oil in a large frying pan over a low heat, add the leeks and chicken livers and cook, stirring, for 5 minutes. Add the peas, ham, nutmeg and the mushrooms and their soaking water and simmer gently for 15 minutes.

Bring a large saucepan of salted water to a boil, add the cappelletti and cook for 1 minute, or until they float to the surface. Quickly drain the pasta and tip it into the saucepan with the leek mixture, adding the cream and Parmesan as you go. Season with salt and pepper to taste.

Preheat the oven to 190°C (375°F), Gas Mark 5. Grease a 25cm (10 inch) pie dish with a little butter.

Roll out the pastry sheets and use one to line the prepared mould, cutting off the excess pastry but leaving a 3-cm (1¼-inch) overhang around the edges. Press along the sides to ensure the pastry adheres well, then fill the mould with the cappelletti and sauce. Cover with the second sheet of dough. Cut off the excess pastry, fold in the overhanging edges and press with your fingertips to close.

Use the remaining pastry to cut out whatever decorative shapes you would like to adorn your pie.

Brush the surface of the pie with the egg yolk and bake in the oven for 30 minutes until the pastry is golden. Leave to cool for 10–15 minutes before serving with a simple green salad.

Polpette della Nonna accompagnate da scalogni glassati
con prugne secche

GRANDMA'S MEATBALLS
WITH GLAZED SHALLOTS & PRUNES

This is one of the first things I ever learnt to make, a scrumptious people-pleaser of a dish – my grandmother's meatballs. There is something dangerously addictive about these mouth-watering morsels, handmade with agile grace. Just try to believe, until #foodhappiness kicks in. If you buy your meat at the butcher, ask him to mince it twice. If not, I suggest you use a sharp knife to chop the mince again yourself, just like you would when chopping herbs.

Preparation time: 25 minutes

Cooking time: 45 minutes

Serves 6

250g (9oz) minced pork

250g (9oz) minced beef sirloin

2 eggs

100g (3¹/₂oz) Parmesan cheese

handful of flat-leaf parsley leaves, finely chopped

50ml (2fl oz) milk

120ml (4fl oz) extra virgin olive oil

150g (5¹/₂oz) breadcrumbs (*see* page 262)

1 garlic clove, peeled and left whole

230ml (8fl oz) dry white wine

salt and pepper

Glazed shallots and prunes:

50g (1³/₄oz) unsalted butter

3 tablespoons extra virgin olive oil

30 banana shallots, peeled

2 tablespoons clear honey

100ml (3¹/₂fl oz) vegetable stock, plus extra if necessary

30 soft pitted prunes, soaked in warm water for 5 minutes, drained and finely chopped

small handful of sage leaves, chopped, plus extra to garnish

For the glazed shallots, gently heat the butter and oil in a large non-stick frying pan, add the shallots and cook for 1 minute, then stir in the honey and leave to cook over a very gentle heat for 30 minutes, occasionally adding a ladleful of stock so that the honey doesn't burn.

While the shallots are cooking, make the meatballs. In a bowl, mix together the minced meats with the eggs, Parmesan, parsley, milk, 2 tablespoons of the extra virgin olive oil, half the breadcrumbs and a pinch each of salt and pepper.

Place the remaining breadcrumbs on a large plate. Take a small handful of the meatball mixture and roll it into a walnut-sized ball, then coat it with breadcrumbs and transfer to a clean dish. Repeat with the remaining meatball mixture. This recipe makes about 40 small meatballs.

Heat the remaining oil in a large heavy-based frying pan over a medium heat. Add the garlic and cook until browned, then carefully place the meatballs in the pan and cook for 2–3 minutes per side until golden brown all over. Remove from the heat and transfer the meatballs to a plate covered with kitchen paper to drain off any excess oil.

Pour the wine into the pan and bring to a vigorous simmer over a high heat. Return the meatballs to the pan and cook for a further 5 minutes until the alcohol has evaporated and the sauce has thickened and reduced to a wonderful golden cream.

To finish the shallots, increase the heat to high, add the prunes and sage and cook, stirring, for 5 minutes until everything has reduced and caramelized.

Serve the meatballs warm or cold alongside the glazed shallots, sprinkling over a little extra chopped sage to finish.

Vitel tonné

TUNA-SAUCED VEAL

The origins of this dish are lost in the mists of time. I like to enjoy it cold, with its luscious sauce spread abundantly on top and adorned with glittering capers. I also like to serve it with puntarelle salad (*see* page 120).

(*see* page 120)

Preparation time: 20 minutes plus chilling

Cooking time: 1 hour 30 minutes

Serves 6

3 tablespoons extra virgin olive oil

1 x 600-g (1-lb 5-oz) organic boneless veal topside

1 celery stick, trimmed

1 carrot, peeled

2 garlic cloves, peeled and left whole

1 large onion, peeled

5 bay leaves

small handful of thyme sprigs

1 rosemary sprig

4 cloves

15 black peppercorns

500ml (18fl oz) dry white wine

500ml (18fl oz) vegetable stock

2 teaspoons salted capers, rinsed, plus extra to garnish

Tuna sauce:

3 hard-boiled eggs, peeled

100g (3½oz) tinned tuna in olive oil, drained

1 teaspoon salted capers, rinsed

6 anchovy fillets

1 tablespoon lemon juice

3 tablespoons extra virgin olive oil

1 tablespoon balsamic vinegar

salt and pepper

Gently heat the olive oil in a large saucepan over a low heat. Lower in the veal together with the vegetables, herbs and spices, pour over the white wine and stock and bring to a gentle simmer. Cover and cook over a low heat for 45 minutes, then remove the lid and cook for a further 45 minutes, until the meat is cooked through and the liquid has reduced by two-thirds.

Once the veal is cooked, carefully remove it from the pan, reserving the cooking liquid, and leave to cool. Once cool, transfer the veal to the refrigerator and leave to chill further for at least 20 minutes (this will firm the meat up and make it easier to slice).

While the veal is chilling, make the tuna sauce. Put all the ingredients except the balsamic vinegar in a food processor and season with salt and pepper to taste. Blend until well combined, then, with the motor running, very gradually add the balsamic vinegar and a little of the veal cooking liquid to form a smooth, thick sauce.

Cut the chilled veal into thin slices, arrange on a serving plate and spoon over the tuna sauce. Top with the capers and serve cold.

Insalata di puntarelle

PUNTARELLE SALAD

Puntarelle is a famously crisp and bitter Roman variant of chicory (in London I buy it at Elsey & Bent in Borough Market or from Natoora, an online supplier). This salad is topped with bocconcini – bite-size mozzarella – and the leaves are dressed with a glorious anchovy sauce (*see* photograph on page 119). Bitter is better.

Preparation time: 15 minutes plus cooling

Serves 6

1 puntarelle (winter chicory) head

4 anchovies in olive oil or
    4 teaspoons anchovy paste

1 garlic clove, peeled and left whole

1 tablespoon white wine vinegar

3 tablespoons extra virgin olive oil

4 tablespoons lemon juice

300g (10½oz) bocconcini

salt and pepper

Cut off and discard the puntarelle base. Cut the leaves in half lengthways and then into thin strips before plunging them into a large bowl of ice cold water. Leave for 1 hour (this will get the leaves nice and crisp and remove some of their bitterness), then pat dry and set aside in a large bowl.

For the dressing, blend the anchovies, garlic, vinegar, oil and lemon juice together in a food processor until well combined and season with salt and pepper to taste.

To finish, mix the puntarelle together with the dressing and scatter over the bocconcini.

Cannelloni al forno con ricotta e zafferano

RICOTTA & SAFFRON CANNELLONI

Gabriele d'Annunzio described the inebriating pleasures of Rome: his most famous novel, *Il Piacere*, published in 1889 and known in English as *The Child of Pleasure*, depicts Roman youth in all its pulsating eccentricities. The same capriciousness is to be found in the city's brilliant architectural bric-a-brac. Rome is a multi-layered city, one element on top of and inside another. Similarly, these cannelloni hold a secret: the translucent ricotta is hidden under a pasta camouflage and its creamy softness adorns the crispy edges.

Preparation time: 30 minutes plus cooling and resting

Cooking time: 50 minutes

Serves 6

4 tablespoons extra virgin olive oil

1 red onion, chopped

300g (10½oz) passata

4 sage leaves

2 red chicory heads, trimmed and leaves chopped

300g (10½oz) ricotta cheese

salt and pepper

Pasta:

300g (10½oz) super-fine grade 00 pasta flour

pinch of salt

3 eggs

Topping:

50g (1¾oz) unsalted butter, softened

100g (3½oz) plain flour

1 litre (1¾ pints) milk

1 teaspoon ground nutmeg

¼ teaspoon saffron threads

50g (1¾oz) breadcrumbs (*see* page 262)

50g (1¾oz) Parmesan cheese, grated

salt and pepper

For the topping, melt the butter in a medium saucepan, then remove from the heat and whisk in the flour to form a paste (roux). Whisking all the while to prevent any lumps forming, gradually add the milk, return the pan to the heat and continue to whisk until the sauce has thickened to the consistency of custard and is gently bubbling. Stir in the nutmeg and saffron, season generously with salt and pepper and set aside for at least 30 minutes to cool.

While the topping is cooling, make the pasta. Pile the flour and salt onto a wooden board or into a bowl, make a well in the centre and crack in the eggs. Whisk the eggs lightly with a fork then, using your hands, mix everything together well to form a rough dough. Knead the dough together until all the pieces have combined and you have formed a velvety smooth lump of dough. (If the dough is looking a little dry, add a few drops of water. If it's too wet, add a little extra flour.) Leave the dough in the refrigerator for at least 30 minutes to rest.

Once rested, divide the dough into 12 equal-sized pieces. Roll each out with a rolling pin on a lightly floured surface to a 7.5 x 15-cm (3 x 6-inch) rectangle. Cover with a damp clean tea towel to prevent the pasta from drying out and set aside.

Preheat the oven to 180°C (350°F), Gas Mark 4.

For the sauce and filling, place two saucepans over a medium heat, adding 2 tablespoons of olive oil and half of the chopped red onion to each. Cook the onion, stirring, for 2–3 minutes until slightly softened, then add the passata and sage leaves to one pan and the chopped chicory to the other. Season both pans with salt and pepper and cook, stirring, for 15 minutes, until the tomato sauce has thickened and reduced slightly and the chicory has softened.

Bring a large saucepan of salted water to a boil. Working in batches, carefully lower the pasta rectangles into the water and cook for 60 seconds, then transfer to a bowl of iced water to prevent them from overcooking (be careful as you go, as the cannelloni are delicate and will tear easily).

Remove the pasta rectangles from the iced water, pat dry with kitchen paper and arrange on a clean work surface. Place a tablespoon of filling along the long edge of a pasta rectangle, then roll up gently to create a tubular shape. Carefully place the cannelloni in the prepared baking dish with the open edges down. Repeat with the remaining pasta rectangles.

Spoon the topping over the cannelloni and sprinkle over the breadcrumbs and Parmesan to finish. Bake in the oven for 25 minutes, or until the topping is golden and bubbling, then leave to cool for 10 minutes before serving.

Coda alla vaccinara in verde

GREEN OXTAIL STEW

Feasting is a universal impulse: it's a way of celebrating your community and your taste buds. Throughout history feasts have also been used to display wealth and power. In the 1st century the Roman Emperor Vitellius amazed his guests by serving ingredients gathered from all corners of the Roman Empire, from dormouse livers to peacock brains. This daring but palatable feast boosted trade across the empire. Offal has never gone out of fashion in the Eternal City. With its deliciously melting consistency, this oxtail is fit for an emperor.

Preparation time: 10 minutes

Cooking time: 2½ hours

Serves 6

1 x 1-kg (2-lb 4-oz) oxtail, cut into 6 slices

1 carrot

2 shallots, 1 peeled and left whole, 1 finely chopped

handful of basil leaves, chopped

handful of sage leaves, chopped

handful of mint leaves, chopped

4 tablespoons extra virgin olive oil

50g (1¾oz) *lardo* (*see* page 158), cut into 1-cm (½-inch) cubes

1 garlic clove, peeled and lightly crushed with the side of a knife

120ml (4fl oz) dry white wine

50g (1¾oz) plain dark chocolate, grated

1 celery stick, trimmed

Celery pesto:

100g (3½oz) celery leaves

50g (1¾oz) pine nuts

1 garlic clove, peeled and lightly crushed with the side of a knife

50g (1¾oz) grated Parmesan cheese

50g (1¾oz) grated pecorino romano cheese

100ml (3½fl oz) extra virgin olive oil

Bring a large saucepan of salted water to a boil. Add the oxtail slices, carrot, whole peeled shallot and half the chopped herb leaves and leave to simmer for 1 hour. Carefully remove the meat with a slotted spoon and set aside, reserving the stock.

Gently heat the olive oil in a large saucepan with the *lardo*. Add the chopped shallot and crushed garlic clove and cook, stirring, for 5 minutes or until the garlic starts to brown.

Remove the garlic clove, add the oxtail slices and cook, stirring, for 2–3 minutes to mix everything together well. Season with salt and pepper, pour over the wine and bring to a simmer, then cover and cook over a medium heat for 45 minutes, stirring occasionally and adding a ladleful of stock whenever necessary to prevent the meat from drying out. Add the celery stick and continue to cook for 45 minutes, stirring, until the oxtail meat begins to fall away from the bones.

While the oxtail is braising, make the pesto. Put the celery leaves, pine nuts, garlic and grated cheeses in a food processor and blend together briefly. Pour over the olive oil and a ladleful of the reserved stock and blend together again to form a smooth paste. Set aside in a small bowl.

Once the oxtail is cooked, remove the meat from the bones, and transfer it to a serving dish (the celery and shallot mixture can be set aside and used as stock for tomorrow's risotto). Spoon over the celery pesto, scatter over the remaining chopped herb leaves and sprinkle over the grated dark chocolate to finish.

Biancomangiare

WHITE SOUP

This dish dates back to the Middle Ages and takes its name from the fact that it consists only of white ingredients. In the Catholic world, the colour white symbolized purity. Most of the churches in Rome are made of white marble, whereas the colour schemes of people's houses go from the light beige of aristocratic palazzos to the earthy orange of the houses inhabited by artisans of all sorts, from the *pizzicagnolo* (specialist grocer) to the shoemaker. Nutritious and slightly sweet, this is a soup traditionally recommended for new mothers and convalescents – Roman food in its oldest and purest form.

Preparation time: 10 minutes

Cooking time: 35 minutes

Serves 4

1.5 litres (2½ pints) water

1 carrot, peeled

1 large tomato

1 large white onion, peeled

1 potato

1 celery stick

200g (7oz) chicken breast fillet

200g (7oz) stale sourdough bread

150ml (¼ pint) milk

10g (¼oz) of salted butter

125g (4½oz) white mushrooms, trimmed and halved

100g (3½oz) ground almonds

50g (1¾oz) fresh root ginger, peeled and grated

200g (7oz) croutons

100g (3½oz) Parmesan cheese, grated

sea salt flakes and pepper

Bring the measured water to a boil in a large saucepan with the carrot, tomato, onion, potato and celery. Add the chicken breast and a small handful of sea salt flakes and poach gently for 20 minutes, then carefully remove the meat with a slotted spoon and leave it to dry between two clean tea towels. Discard the vegetables and set the stock aside.

Place the bread in a large serving bowl, cover with the milk and leave to soak.

Melt a little butter in a frying pan over a medium heat, add the mushrooms and sauté for 10 minutes until softened and lightly golden.

Remove the mushrooms from the pan and leave to cool, then roughly chop them together with the chicken meat and mix them with the stale bread, almonds and ginger to form a creamy mush. Transfer to a blender and blitz until smooth.

Return the stock to a boil.

When ready to serve, add a ladleful of the boiling stock to the bowl containing the chicken mixture to get a soupy consistency and scatter over the croutons. Pour over the remaining stock, stir everything together well and season with salt and pepper. Sprinkle over the Parmesan and serve immediately.

Chapter 5

APERITIVO

The working day is finally over. Everybody is out in the streets, enjoying the last rays of the incredible orange Roman sun that has the power to light up all buildings, cupolas and hearts. The scent of incense and flowers pervades the air, while artisans and *gelatai* alike yawn the end of the day away. What started off at the beginning of the afternoon as an innocent daydream and a vague desire to chill out with your friends after work has now swiftly turned into a vital need for a drink. In Rome, it's time for the *aperitivo*.

A relatively new social phenomenon, the *aperitivo* is characterized by booze, food that is easy on the mouth, and plenty of good conversation. It usually starts after working hours and can last until 9pm, or all night long, depending on the temperature outside and the number of people who have assembled to chat, discuss and argue the evening away. It's also just another way to consume a light dinner. Most respectable bars will have a counter dedicated to all things edible designed to accompany a tantalizing drink, usually including arancini, Tramezzini (*see* page 146), rice salads, *crocchette* (*see* page 134), cheeses, *supplì* (*see* page 134), Panzanella (*see* page 132), Alici Marinate (*see* page 147) and anything else that might put a smile on the eater's face.

Behind the Piazza Navona in Rome, there's a bar called Bar del Fico. Old folks with expressive bristly moustaches and unshakeable optimism, who still live in this historic neighbourhood, gather to play chess under the trees that decorate a tiny square. You can see them concentrating on the game, surrounded by a crowd made up of people of all ages with a Negroni (*see* page 268) in one hand and a cigarette lighter in the other, talking in raspy voices, almost seeming to grate out the words. I'm inclined to think that it must have taken a lot of cigarettes, smoked in an exceptionally heartfelt style, together with the strategic Roman art of being actively lazy, to produce these particular voices. They're keen to predict the next move in the game of chess, all overjoyed astonishment and amiable severity, while also talking about the latest blockbuster movie or 'deciding on' their football team's line-up for the next match. It's not just all about women and cars.

Mozzarella in carrozza

MOZZARELLA IN A CARRIAGE

Rome is the title of a brief and enchanting unfinished work by the 19th-century Russian novelist Nikolai Gogol. He talks of how during Carnival season, carriages were filled with people of all classes, their faces covered with flour and beaming with joy, for once mixing with each other – for the rest of the year, the division would be rather more brutal. In this recipe, the 'carriage' is filled with cheese. Use fully drained *mozzarella da cucina*, the most basic cooking mozzarella, which you can find in any supermarket – it's also the cheese to use for your *pizzette* (*see* page 55).

Preparation time: 5 minutes

Cooking time: 5 minutes

Serves 6

12 white or brown bread slices, crusts removed and cut into quarters

150g (5½oz) *mozzarella da cucina* (cooking mozzarella), cut into 5-mm (⅛-inch) slices

1 x 100-g (3½-oz) jar of anchovy fillets in olive oil, drained

small handful of rosemary leaves

100ml (3½fl oz) milk

100g (3½oz) plain flour

2 eggs

100ml (3½fl oz) vegetable oil

Arrange the bread quarters on a large plate or a clean work surface. Place a slice of mozzarella, 1 anchovy fillet and a few rosemary leaves on half of the bread quarters, then use the remaining bread quarters to sandwich together.

Pour the milk into one shallow bowl and the flour into another. Beat the eggs and tip into a third bowl.

Take the sandwiches, one by one, and dunk them first into the milk, then dredge them in the flour, then dip them in the beaten egg.

Heat the oil in a large frying pan over a medium heat, carefully add the sandwiches and cook for about 1 minute on each side until crisp and golden (you may have to do this in batches depending on the size of your pan). Drain briefly on kitchen paper and serve straight away.

Panzanella

BREAD SALAD

In the mild mid-summer evenings, I walk around the narrow streets of this splendid city, my ears pricked for the ever-present sound of a mandolin. I'm right at home as I walk past the Pantheon through Piazza della Rotonda, which truly feels like a large living room to me. Who needs to visit art galleries when you have an open-air museum at your feet? I like to make myself this salad and have an impromptu picnic sitting on a marble bench, never bored with having my breath taken away. Improvisation – that's how I summer.

Preparation time: 10 minutes plus resting

Cooking time: 5 minutes

Serves 4

4 tablespoons extra virgin olive oil

200g (7oz) rustic bread loaf, torn into bite-sized pieces

4 firm tomatoes

2 large red onions, peeled

1 cucumber, cut into 2-cm (3/4-inch) cubes

1 celery stick, trimmed and cut into 2-cm (3/4-inch) cubes

15 pitted black olives, finely chopped

40g (1 1/2oz) rocket leaves, finely chopped

small handful of basil leaves, finely chopped

20ml (3/4fl oz) white or red wine vinegar

100g (3 1/2oz) pecorino romano cheese, cut into 2-cm (3/4-inch) cubes

salt and pepper

Heat 2 tablespoons of olive oil in a large non-stick frying pan over a high heat. Add the bread pieces and fry, turning occasionally, for 5 minutes until crisp and golden all over. Remove from the heat and set aside.

Place the tomatoes in a bowl and pour over boiling water to cover. Leave for 1–2 minutes, then drain, cut a cross at the stem end of each tomato, and peel off the skins. Cut the tomatoes roughly into 5-mm (1/4-inch) cubes, discarding the seeds.

Slice the onions and place them in a bowl of cold water for 10 minutes. Drain and dry on a clean tea towel.

In a salad bowl, mix together the sliced onions, chopped cucumbers, celery, tomatoes and olives, then add the chopped rocket and basil leaves, pour over the vinegar and the remaining 2 tablespoons of oil and season with salt and pepper. Finish the panzanella by adding the toasted bread pieces and giving everything a final gentle mix to ensure the bread is covered in all the juices. This salad is delicious served immediately, or you can keep it in the refrigerator for up to 3 days, letting it absorb the mix of aromatic flavours. Scatter over the pecorino before serving.

FRITTER TRIO OF ROMAN-STYLE RICE BALLS, POTATO CROQUETTES & MINI MEAT LOAVES

Bernini and Borromini shared between them the most desirable sculptural and architectural commissions to be carried out in Rome in the 17th century, yet rumour has it they were fierce enemies. On Piazza Navona, you'll see Borromini's Church of Sant'Agnese in Agone. Facing it is Bernini's fountain of the Four Rivers. Allegedly, Bernini designed two of the fountain's four allegorical figures to make fun of his rival: one with his hand raised to protect himself from the building's imminent collapse, and the other with his head hidden under a veil in disgust. Sacred and profane, history and legend – in other words, *fritto misto all'italiana*.

Preparation time: 50 minutes plus chilling

Cooking time: 1¼ hours

Serves 4

5 eggs, beaten

400g (14oz) breadcrumbs (*see* page 262)

50g (1¾oz) plain flour

400ml (14fl oz) vegetable oil

Supplì:

2 tablespoons extra virgin olive oil

1 x 300-g (10½-oz) veal brain, cleaned and chopped

250g (9oz) passata (sieved tomatoes)

120ml (4fl oz) red wine

small handful of flat-leaf parsley leaves, chopped

500ml (18fl oz) beef stock

40g (1½oz) unsalted butter

1 small white onion, chopped

400g (14oz) risotto rice

100g (3½oz) Parmesan cheese, grated

1 egg, beaten

200g (7oz) Fontina cheese, cut into 3-cm (1¼-inch) strips

For the potato croquettes, put the mashed potato in a bowl together with the thyme, Parmesan and the beaten egg and mix together well. Leave in the refrigerator to cool.

For the *supplì*, warm the oil over a low heat in a medium casserole dish. Add the veal brain and cook, stirring, for 10 minutes until the brain pieces are almost melted, then add the passata and wine. Increase the heat to medium and cook for a further 30 minutes, adding the parsley halfway through cooking, until the sauce has thickened and reduced.

Warm the beef stock in a saucepan. Melt half the butter in a medium saucepan, add the onion and fry for 5 minutes until softened. Add the rice, increase the heat to high and cook, stirring, for 2–3 minutes until the rice is translucent. Lower the heat and keep stirring while adding the warm stock gradually, allowing each ladleful to be absorbed before adding the next, for 12–15 minutes or until the rice is plump and tender. Remove the rice from the heat and add the Parmesan, beaten egg and remaining butter and stir gently to combine. Stir in the tomato sauce and season with salt and pepper, then spoon the mixture into a large serving dish. Transfer to the refrigerator to chill and firm.

For the meat loaves, bring a large saucepan of salted water to a boil. Add the onion, celery, carrot, beef and chicken, reduce to a simmer and cook for 1 hour over a low heat. Lift the meat out of the stock with a slotted spoon and leave to cool, then tip it into into a food processor with the soaked bread, garlic, mortadella, Parmesan, parsley, lemon zest, rosemary, nutmeg and beaten egg and blend together well, then stir in the mashed potato and season with salt and pepper. Using your hands, shape the mixture into 4-cm (1½-inch) balls, then pat each with your palm to form flattened loaves.

Potato croquettes:

800g (1lb 12oz) Maris Piper floury potatoes, baked until tender then mashed

small handful of thyme leaves

120g (4oz) Parmesan cheese, grated

1 large egg, beaten

60g (2¼oz) *mozzarella da cucina* (cooking mozzarella), cut into 3-cm (1¼-inch) strips

60g (2¼oz) roast ham, cut into 3-cm (1¼-inch) strips

salt and pepper

Meat loaves:

1 small onion, peeled

1 celery stick, trimmed

1 small carrot, peeled

150g (5½oz) beef

150g (5½oz) chicken breast, cut into chunks

100g (3½oz) stale bread, soaked in 130ml (4fl oz) milk

1 garlic clove, peeled and left whole

50g (1¾oz) mortadella

50g (1¾oz) Parmesan cheese, grated

handful of flat-leaf parsley leaves, chopped

zest of 1 lemon

1 teaspoon dried rosemary

1 teaspoon ground nutmeg

1 large egg, beaten

1 x 200-g (7-oz) Maris Piper floury potato, baked until tender then mashed

salt

Now form the *supplì* and potato croquettes. For the *supplì*, take a strip of Fontina, form a little ball of rice around it and squeeze it into a sausage shape. Repeat with the remaining cheese and rice. For the croquettes, take a piece of mozzarella and a piece of ham, form a little ball of mashed potato around it and squeeze it into a sausage shape. Repeat with the remaining cheese, ham and potatoes.

Pour the beaten eggs, breadcrumbs and flour into three separate bowls. Dip the potato croquettes and meat loaves in the flour, then into the beaten egg and finally into the breadcrumbs to coat evenly. Dip the *supplì* in the eggs and then into the breadcrumbs.

Heat the oil in a large, heavy-based saucepan or deep-fryer until 180–190°C (350–375°F) or until a cube of bread browns in 30 seconds. Carefully add the *supplì*, croquettes and meat loaves in batches and cook for 1–2 minutes per side until golden brown all over. Remove from the oil with a slotted spoon and drain on kitchen paper. Serve warm and tantalizingly crispy.

Olive all'ascolana

ASCOLI-STYLE STUFFED OLIVES

In Rome, blue cars mean a special category of people, who can use dedicated routes and park wherever they like. These blue cars should be a privilege of government elites, but it doesn't take long to realize that the person you saw jumping a red light was not an important politician, but the friend of a cousin of the Minister's secretary. Nunzio, the barman, tells me: *Bella signorina*, it's all about who you know.' As I understand it, once you know 'the right people', you can go a long way in Rome, at least without ever having to take a bus... These round, golden morsels are so good they must be illegal somewhere, but surely not around here. Nepotism, a glass of bubbly and stuffed olives.

Preparation time: 20 minutes plus chilling

Cooking time: 30 minutes

Serves 4

2 tablespoons extra virgin olive oil

1 small carrot, finely chopped

1 small onion, finely chopped

50g (1³/₄oz) pancetta or smoked bacon, finely chopped

1 celery stick, trimmed and finely chopped

100g (3¹/₂oz) minced beef

100g (3¹/₂oz) minced pork

100g (3¹/₂oz) minced chicken

100ml (3¹/₂fl oz) dry white wine

150ml (¹/₄ pint) vegetable stock

zest of ¹/₂ lemon

60g (2¹/₄oz) Parmesan cheese, grated

1 teaspoon ground nutmeg

1 garlic clove, peeled

2 eggs

150g (5¹/₂oz) breadcrumbs (*see* page 262)

60 large green olives, pitted

50g (1³/₄oz) plain flour

300ml (¹/₂ pint) vegetable oil

salt

Heat the oil over a low heat in a large frying pan, add the carrot, onion, pancetta and celery and cook, stirring, for 5 minutes, until the vegetables have softened. Add the minced meats and cook gently, stirring occasionally, for 10 minutes, until browned all over, then add the wine and stock, bring to a vigorous simmer and cook for a further 10 minutes, or until the liquids have evaporated.

Remove the pan from the heat and transfer the contents to a food processor. Add the lemon zest, Parmesan, nutmeg, clove, 1 egg and one-third of the breadcrumbs and mix everything together to form a smooth, soft paste. Season with salt to taste.

Spoon the filling into a piping bag with a small nozzle attached and squeeze the filling into the olives.

Arrange the flour in one shallow bowl and the remaining breadcrumbs in another. Beat the remaining egg and tip it into a third bowl. Roll the stuffed olives first in flour, then in the egg, then in the breadcrumbs. Transfer the olives to the refrigerator to chill for 20 minutes, then repeat the dipping process to ensure a thorough coating.

Heat the vegetable oil in a large, heavy-based saucepan or deep-fryer to 180–190°C (350–375°F) or until a cube of bread browns in 30 seconds. Carefully add the olives and cook for 1–2 minutes per side until golden brown all over. Remove from the oil with a slotted spoon and drain on kitchen paper. Serve warm.

Fiori di zucca ripieni

STUFFED COURGETTE FLOWERS

For as long as I can remember courgette flowers have been one the main protagonists of the Roman food scene. Yes, their pistils and stamens need to be meticulously removed before you can eat them, but don't be put off. Beyond their apparently hard-to-handle appearance, these delectable blossoms are soft yet crunchy, perfectly suited for frying as well as for making a delicious pizza topping. In this recipe they are stuffed with a mix of glorious cheeses. Accompany the stuffed flowers with a glass of Chianti for a perfect little starter.

Preparation time: 15 minutes

Cooking time: 5 minutes

Serves 4

extra virgin olive oil, for greasing

12 large courgette flowers

250g (9oz) ricotta cheese

100g (3½oz) Taleggio, Fontina or other semi-soft cheese

1 teaspoon ground nutmeg

1 teaspoon white pepper

3 tablespoons grated Parmesan cheese

50g (1¾oz) breadcrumbs (*see* page 262)

salt

Preheat the oven to 180°C (350°F), Gas Mark 4. Lightly oil a large baking tray.

Using a sharp knife, cut away any bumpy growths around the base of each courgette flower and trim away the majority of the stem, leaving about 1cm (½ inch) attached (this will not only help keep the flowers together but will also look pretty). Gently cut open the courgette flowers lengthways, being careful not to break them, and remove the stamens or pistils. Alternatively, instead of cutting open the flowers, gently peel apart the petals, being careful not to tear them.

In a bowl, mix together the ricotta, Taleggio, nutmeg and white pepper with half the Parmesan and season with salt.

Using either a piping bag or a teaspoon, carefully fill the courgette flowers with the cheese mixture. Close the flowers, twisting the ends of the petals to seal, then transfer to the prepared baking tray. Scatter over the breadcrumbs and the remaining Parmesan and bake in the oven for 5 minutes until the courgette flowers are lightly golden. Serve warm.

CHICKEN GALANTINE WITH CHEESY GRAPES

Galantina di pollo servita con bocconcini d'uva al formaggio

Preparation time: 30 minutes plus marinating and chilling

Cooking time: 2 hours 25 minutes

Serves 8

100g veal topside, cut into 2-cm (½-inch) chunks

200g (7oz) pork loin, cut into 2-cm (½-inch) chunks

100g (3½oz) mortadella

100g (3½oz) prosciutto

500ml (18fl oz) Marsala wine

3 litres (5¼ pints) water

1 carrot

1 celery stick, trimmed

1 vine tomato

1 potato

1 large white onion, studded with 6 cloves

1 egg

large handful of dried porcini mushrooms (ceps)

1 x 1.5-kg (3-lb 5-oz) free range chicken, boned

200g (7oz) unsalted pistachios, roughly chopped

4 black summer truffles, roughly chopped

sea salt flakes

Cheesy grapes:

150g (5oz) unsalted pistachios, coarsely chopped

100g (3½oz) Gorgonzola cheese

100g (3½oz) cream cheese

small bunch of seedless green grapes

One of the world's first cookbooks, compiled in the 4th century and named *Apicius* after a Roman gourmet, includes a recipe for stuffed chicken, a dish prepared for superb banquets. This recipe for chicken galantine is a little elaborate but you will be so pleased with the result. The whole process of tying up the chicken and simmering it in stock is rather reminiscent of a time gone by that we should try to hold on to. Tradition in evolution. Try it to believe it.

Place the veal and pork pieces together with the mortadella and prosciutto in a large bowl, pour over the Marsala and leave to marinate for 30 minutes.

Meanwhile, bring the measured water to a boil in a large saucepan with the carrot, celery, tomato, potato and clove-studded onion. Add a small handful of sea salt flakex, reduce the heat and simmer gently, covered, for 25 minutes.

Remove the meat pieces from the marinade and transfer to a food processor along with the egg , porcini mushrooms and a pinch of salt. Blend everything together to mince the meat and form a thick, creamy paste.

Lay the chicken on a board skin-side down and spread the creamy meat mixture over the top. Scatter over the pistachios and truffles and roll up into a fat log, tucking in the ends as you roll. Place on a clean tea towel and roll up tightly, then tie the chicken in three or four places with kitchen string to help it keep its shape and ensure even cooking, trimming off any extra string around your knots.

Immerse the chicken in the stock, cover with a lid and leave to simmer over a low heat for 2 hours.

While the chicken is simmering, make the cheesy grapes. Put the chopped pistachios in a bowl. In a second bowl, mix both cheeses together with a whisk until light and creamy. Dip the grapes on their stems first into the cheese mix and then into the pistachios to coat evenly, then transfer to the refrigerator and leave to chill.

Once the galantine is ready, remove it from the stock and transfer it to the refrigerator for at least 4 hours to chill and set (alternatively you could place it in the freezer for 1½ hours if you're in a hurry, just don't forget it's there!).

When ready to serve, remove the strings from the chicken and cut it into thin slices. Arrange on a serving dish and garnish with the cheesy grapes.

Sandwich di polenta con salsiccia e formaggio

POLENTA SANDWICH
WITH BAKED SAUSAGE & CHEESE

I'm going slightly off track here with polenta, a staple of northern Italy. Originally made in huge portions, this golden cornmeal porridge was then spread out on wooden slabs and topped with sausage. *La morte sua* – to die for. It's still considered a *cibo povero* today – a pocket- as well as a crowd-pleaser – and you can now find little polenta snacks during the *aperitivo* hour in Rome.

Preparation time: 20 minutes plus cooling

Cooking time: 3 minutes

Makes 15 sandwiches

unsalted butter, for greasing

approx. 1.5 litres (2½ pints) water (check polenta package instructions for exact quantities)

250g (9oz) quick-cook polenta

4 pork sausages

2 tablespoons extra virgin olive oil

150g (5½oz) Fontina, provolone or Bel Paese cheese, thinly sliced

small handful of thyme leaves

sea salt flakes

Preheat the oven to 190°C (375°F), Gas Mark 5. Grease a 39 x 26-cm (15¼ x 10½-inch) oven tray with butter and line a baking tray with baking paper.

To make the polenta, bring the water to a boil together with a handful of salt. Gradually add the polenta, stirring with a wooden spoon, and cook, stirring continuously, for 5 minutes. Remove from the heat and stir for a further 4–5 minutes, until the polenta has thickened but still remains easy to pour.

Pour the polenta into the prepared oven tray and flatten it with a spatula into a 2-cm (¾-inch) thick layer. Leave to cool and set for 30 minutes.

While the polenta is cooling, arrange the sausages in a baking dish, drizzle over the oil and bake for 30 minutes. Let the sausages cool for 10 minutes, then cut each into 10–12 slices to obtain 45 slices in total (3 per sandwich).

Cut the cooled polenta into thirty 5 x 2.5-cm (2 x 1-inch) rectangles or use the rim of a sherry glass to form the same number of polenta circles.

Arrange half the polenta pieces on the prepared baking tray. Top each of the arranged polenta pieces with the sausage and cheese slices and sandwich together with a second polenta piece. Bake for 10 minutes, until crisp and golden. Transfer to a serving dish, scatter over the thyme and serve.

These mouth-watering morsels will keep in the refrigerator for up to 3 days: simply reheat them in a low oven for a few minutes at 150°C (300°F), Gas Mark 2.

TEA SANDWICHES

The idea of stuffing bread – or making sandwiches – dates back to imperial Rome. Over the last 20 years, however, the *tramezzino* has become an expression of gastronomic creativity, with infinite fillings. Paired with a glass of local aperitif, these soft sandwiches have become a part of the Italian lifestyle – this particular example is reminiscent of the Italian flag.

Preparation time: 25 minutes plus resting

Serves 8

4 slices white sandwich bread, crusts removed

4 slices wholemeal bread, crusts removed

White cream filling:

handful of rosemary leaves, finely chopped

handful of thyme leaves, finely chopped

handful of basil leaves, finely chopped

250g (9oz) cream cheese

Green cream filling:

150g (5½oz) rocket leaves

4–5 tablespoons extra virgin olive oil

70g (2½oz) pine nuts

100g (3½oz) Parmesan cheese, grated

100g (3½oz) pecorino romano cheese, grated

2 garlic cloves, peeled and left whole

pinch of salt

Red cream filling:

100g (3½oz) smoked salmon

handful of dill fronds

150g (5½oz) ricotta cheese

2 tablespoons tomato purée

Line a 900g (2lb) loaf tin with clingfilm.

To prepare the white cream filling, stir the chopped herbs through the cream cheese in a bowl. Set aside.

To prepare the green cream filling, put the rocket leaves and a little of the olive oil in a food processor with the rest of the ingredients. Blend together, gradually adding the remaining oil until you reach a creamy consistency. Set aside.

To prepare the red cream filling, blend the salmon, dill, ricotta and tomato purée together in the food processor to form a smooth, creamy paste.

To assemble the sandwich loaf, arrange 2 wholemeal bread slices, trimming as necessary, to form a layer on the bottom of the loaf tin. Spread over the red cream filling evenly using a spatula, then cover with 2 white bread slices. Spread the white cream filling over evenly in the same way, then cover again with wholemeal bread slices and spread over the green cream filling. Finish with the final 2 slices of white bread.

Wrap the tin with clingfilm and transfer to the refrigerator for 2 hours for everything to rest (if you're in a hurry you can do this in the freezer – it'll only take 30 minutes – just don't forget about it!).

Once the sandwich loaf has rested, remove the clingfilm, invert the tin and cut it into 2-cm (¾-inch) slices. Enjoy with a glass of sparkling prosecco.

Alici o sardine marinate

MARINATED ANCHOVIES OR SARDINES

Go to your fishmonger to buy a silvery grey multitude of fresh anchovies or sardines – they are good for you. Ask him to remove the heads and the backbones, because there is no denying that having to prepare these little fish yourself is a pain. Your fishmonger will do it for you, with pleasure, as long as he isn't rushed off his feet – on a busy Saturday morning, forget it!

Preparation time: 10 minutes plus soaking

Cooking time: 30 minutes

Serves 8

500g (1lb 2oz) fresh anchovies or sardines, heads and backbones removed (ask your fishmonger to do this for you)

300ml (½ pint) white wine vinegar

5 tablespoons extra virgin olive oil, plus extra for greasing

150g (5½oz) breadcrumbs (*see* page 262)

150g (5½oz) pecorino romano cheese, grated

2 garlic cloves, grated

large handful of flat-leaf parsley leaves, very finely chopped

30g (1oz) dried oregano

salt and pepper

Place the anchovies in a bowl, cover with the vinegar and leave to soak for 15 minutes.

Preheat the oven to 180°C (350°F), Gas Mark 4. Grease a baking dish with a little olive oil.

Sprinkle the breadcrumbs over the base of the baking dish in an even layer, then arrange a layer of anchovies on top and season with salt and pepper. Continue to layer the anchovies alternately with layers of the cheese, grated garlic, chopped parsley and oregano, seasoning as you go and finishing with a layer of anchovy fillets. Pour over the olive oil and bake in the oven for 30 minutes until golden.

Enjoy the anchovies warm or cold as an *aperitivo* or use as an alternative topping for bruschetta (*see* page 46).

Limoni ripieni alla crema di tonno

LEMONS FILLED WITH TUNA CREAM

In a favourable climate, lemon trees flower and bear fruit four times a year. Therefore this festive citrus dish can be found on our tables all year round. The creamy filling reminds me of the more famous Pesce Finto di Natale (*see* page 222), but with the addition of mascarpone cheese. Italians like variations, after all, hardly ever sticking to a fixed plan. This luminous dish resonates with rural tradition, a nod to the little details that make life a marvellous journey. *Bella la vita, eh?*

Preparation time: 20 minutes plus chilling

Serves 4

4 large unwaxed lemons

180g (6oz) tinned tuna in olive oil, drained

2 teaspoons salted capers, rinsed

90g (3¼oz) mayonnaise

50g (1¾oz) mascarpone cheese

50g (1¾oz) pitted black olives

3 hard-boiled eggs, peeled

small handful of chives

small handful of dill fronds

½ teaspoon dried oregano

pinch of salt

pinch of white pepper

pinch of chilli flakes

To garnish

1 tablespoon chopped chives

1 tablespoon chopped dill fronds

½ teaspoon dried oregano

Halve the lemons lengthways.

Squeeze 4 tablespoons of juice out of one lemon and set this aside, then scoop out the pulp from all the lemons using a teaspoon. Remove and discard the seeds and put the lemon pulp and reserved juice in a food processor together with the rest of the ingredients. Blend together well to form a thick, creamy paste.

Use a spoon or a piping bag to fill the empty lemon halves, then scatter over the chopped herbs and dried oregano to finish. The filled lemons can be stored in the refrigerator for up to 3 days until needed.

Chapter 6 ROMANTIC DINNERS

Anyone keen to seek out authentic Roman types should make a note of the term '*coatto*'. A *coatto* is the guy you see passing the time in the local bar or square. Restless by nature, irritated by what he perceives to be the inescapable monotony of life, he harbours strong reactions to even the most inconsequential events. He has a passion for sports in general (and for motorbikes and souped-up cars in particular), wears flashy clothes and talks with his hands, his exaggerated gestures accompanied by laughter louder than his car stereo. He performs hilarious acts of bravado, showing off like an urban peacock for the benefit of his girlfriend and the amusement of his pals. Don't mistake his behaviour for rudeness or malice; in most cases it's just the result of a misplaced lust for life and hides a good heart and a fierce sense of loyalty.

Like the majority of their countrymen, Romans don't move out of their parents' homes until they are well into their thirties. I guess *mamma*'s gnocchi are just too good to leave behind. In Italy, leaving home usually involves not only a car filled with boxes but also a precious notebook of old recipes from *nonna*, to bring out on those special occasions, like a romantic dinner. Don't panic, tradition is your saviour here – after all, the best way to someone's heart is through their stomach. Every mouthful has to be delicious. Whatever you decide to cook, *don't* make it like their mother would. You could never compete. Instead, whip out those tricks you learnt from your grandma and pull it off the Roman way, by giving tradition a glossy, modern finish. Surprise them with the crispiness of Orata in Crosta di Patate (*see* page 161), assail their senses with crunchy lamb *costolette*, cauliflower and chestnuts (*see* page 164), or embrace them with the warmth of pasta and chickpeas (*see* page 158).

Working your magic through food is a proven path to success, for both you and your guest – think of the lavish banquets of Ancient Rome, where people used to lie on their sides, lazily picking at food in a position that had the advantage of letting them doze off between courses, while the harmonious singing of the muses created a dinner scenario somewhere between reality and imagination. That's where we are headed in this chapter: romantic food to let the magic happen. Tempting and easy. Impossibly delicious.

Bucatini alle vongole e patate alla menta

BUCATINI WITH CLAMS & MINTY POTATOES

The real value of an ingredient lies in its quality – particularly true with a dish like this one. To make this saucy paradise, I visit my fishmonger and, with exquisite stubbornness, ask for the freshest clams. Once I'm home, the first thing I do is check them for sand. Arm yourself with the same devoted patience you show your significant other and tap each clam, with the opening facing down, against a cutting board. If dark sand comes out, throw the clam away. Also, get rid of those with broken shells – you only want the best. After all, it's romance you're after. This dish is best served piping hot.

Preparation time: 20 minutes plus soaking

Cooking time: 30 minutes

Serves 2

1 Charlotte potato or other waxy potato, peeled

500g (1lb 2oz) fresh clams

2 tablespoons extra virgin olive oil

2 garlic cloves, peeled and left whole

knob of unsalted butter

small handful of mint leaves, very finely chopped

150g (5½oz) bucatini or spaghetti

handful of flat-leaf parsley leaves, finely chopped

1 teaspoon salted capers, rinsed, to garnish

salt and pepper

To remove excess starch from the potato, peel it and leave it to soak in a bowl of water for 15 minutes, then drain it and cut it into 5-mm (¼-inch) cubes.

Meanwhile, put the clams in a colander and rinse them well under running water. Drain well and set aside.

Gently heat 1 tablespoon of olive oil in a large saucepan. Add one whole garlic clove and leave for 2–3 minutes to brown, then tip in the clams, cover with the lid and cook over a high heat for 5 minutes, or until the clams are completely open. Remove from the heat and drain the clams in a colander over a bowl, reserving the precious cooking liquid. Extract the clam meat from half of the shells and discard any clams that haven't opened.

Add the potato cubes to a small saucepan of salted water, bring to a simmer and cook over a medium-high heat for 10 minutes until tender, then drain. Melt a little butter in the same pan, add the potato pieces along with the mint, season to taste and cook for a further 5 minutes until the potatoes have softened further and the flavours have mingled together.

Bring a large saucepan of salted water to a boil, add the pasta and cook according to the packet instructions until al dente, then drain, reserving a few ladlefuls of the pasta cooking water.

While the pasta is cooking, heat the remaining olive oil in another large saucepan with the remaining whole garlic clove for 2–3 minutes until the garlic clove has browned, then pour over the clam cooking liquid, bring to a simmer and cook for roughly 5 minutes or until reduced by half.

Add the drained pasta to the pan along with the shelled clams, minty potatoes and parsley, then gradually add the reserved pasta cooking water along with the remaining clams still in their shells. Spoon into bowls and scatter over the capers to garnish.

Ossobuco al pepe verde e vignarola

ROMAN-STYLE OSSOBUCO WITH VIGNAROLA

Preparation time: 15 minutes

Cooking time: 2 hours 20 minutes

Serves 2

50g (1³/₄oz) plain flour

2 organic veal shin pieces, about 4cm (1¹/₂ inches) thick

2 tablespoons dried green peppercorns

1 small carrot, peeled

1 shallot, peeled

1 celery stick, trimmed

2 anchovies in olive oil

zest of 1 lemon

10 sage leaves

3 tablespoons extra virgin olive oil

50g (1³/₄oz) unsalted butter

120ml (4fl oz) dry white wine

250ml (9fl oz) vegetable stock

Vignarola:

3 tablespoons extra virgin olive oil

10g (¹/₄oz) unsalted butter

2 spring onions, chopped

100g (3¹/₂oz) pancetta or smoked bacon cubes

200g (7oz) broad beans or edamame, defrosted if frozen

100g (3¹/₂oz) garden peas, defrosted if frozen

3 large artichokes, cleaned (*see* page 13), cut into 1-cm (¹/₂-inch) slices and placed in acidulated water

150g (5¹/₂oz) romaine lettuce, chopped

handful of mint leaves

120ml (4fl oz) vegetable stock

50g (1³/₄oz) pecorino romano cheese, grated

salt

In a tiny side street off the imposing Via della Scrofa, there's a restaurant called La Campana. It's one of the oldest in Rome, dating back to 1518, when it offered board and travel booking services to pilgrims and foreigners. Their *vignarola* is a gift from heaven – hands down the best I've ever tasted. This stew of spring vegetables is a reminder of the unbelievable awesomeness of every little thing. There are few better things in life than dunking bread into a plate of ossobuco. This dish is a perennial favourite with lovers of Roman cuisine.

Place the flour in a plastic food bag, add the veal shin pieces and shake to coat.

Lightly crush the peppercorns in a pestle and mortar or with the flat side of a heavy knife and press them into the veal pieces.

Put the carrot, shallot and celery in a food processor and blend together briefly until finely chopped. Set the mixture aside and repeat with the anchovies, lemon zest and sage.

Heat the oil and butter in a casserole dish over a medium heat until the butter has melted. Lower in the veal pieces and brown for 2–3 minutes on each side, then pour over the wine, bring to a vigorous simmer and cook for 15 minutes, until the liquid has evaporated. Pour over the vegetable stock, lower the heat to a gentle simmer and leave to cook, covered, for about 2 hours, until the meat is falling off the bone.

While the ossobuco is cooking, prepare the *vignarola*. Heat the oil and butter together in a large frying pan over a medium heat, add the spring onions and pancetta and cook, stirring, for 3–4 minutes until translucent. Add the broad beans, peas, artichoke slices, chopped lettuce and half of the mint, then pour over the stock, bring to a simmer and cook for 15–20 minutes, or until the liquid has reduced by half. Season with salt and scatter over the grated pecorino to finish.

To serve, transfer the veal pieces onto plates and pour over the juices from the dish. Spoon over the anchovy mixture, scatter with the remaining mint leaves and serve accompanied by the *vignarola*.

Pasta e ceci, salvia e fagioli del purgatorio con tartufo nero e lardo

PASTA, CHICKPEAS & BEANS
WITH BLACK TRUFFLES & LARDO

In Rome, you might bump into a *commendatore* – a guy who acts as if he's entitled to the honours of a knight but without carrying out any of the duties. He always seems to be on to the next big deal in town, mentioning it 'discreetly' to his trusted waiter, who in turn will barely mention it to the barber, a very reliable man who's married to the grocer. 'Shhh, no one knows about it, *capo!*' he'll mutter, flashing his gold teeth. Then he'll turn to his bowl of *pasta e ceci*. This is an everyday dish turned into a special treat by adding black summer truffles and *lardo di Colonnata*, a cured piece of hard fat. You can find good *lardo* in Italian delis and online.

Preparation time: 10 minutes

Cooking time: 45 minutes

Serves 2

40g (1½oz) *lardo di Colonnata* or other good-quality *lardo*, thinly sliced

4 tablespoons extra virgin olive oil

1 garlic clove, peeled and lightly crushed with a heavy knife

1 small carrot, very finely chopped

1 shallot, very finely chopped

1 celery stick, trimmed and very finely chopped

1 teaspoon dried rosemary

30g (1oz) pancetta or smoked bacon cubes

50ml (2fl oz) white wine

100g (3½oz) canned cannellini beans, drained

100g (3½oz) canned chickpeas, drained

150g (5½oz) passata

100ml (3½fl oz) vegetable stock

1 bay leaf

20g (¾oz) black summer truffles, cleaned and cut into thin slices

150g (5½oz) chifferi rigati, ditalini or any other short pasta

salt and pepper

Heat the *lardo* in a small non-stick frying pan over a medium heat for 5 minutes until crispy and crunchy. Set aside.

Gently heat the oil and crushed garlic clove together in a medium saucepan for 2–3 minutes, then remove the garlic clove and add the chopped carrot, shallot, celery and rosemary. Cook for 5 minutes, stirring occasionally, then add the pancetta and cook for a further 5 minutes until the vegetables have started to soften. Add the wine, beans and chickpeas, increase the heat and simmer vigorously for 10 minutes until the liquid has evaporated.

Add the passata, stock and bay leaf to the pan, bring to a gentle simmer and cook for a further 20 minutes or until reduced by half. Transfer half the mixture to a food processor and blend to a smooth purée-like consistency. Return to the pan, stir in half of the truffle slices and season with salt and pepper. Keep warm.

Bring a large saucepan of salted water to a boil, add the pasta and cook according to the packet instructions until al dente.

Drain the pasta and mix it together with the sauce. Ladle into 2 shallow bowls, scatter over the crunchy *lardo* pieces and remaining truffle slices and serve piping hot.

Orata in crosta di patate

SEABREAM IN A POTATO CRUST

One of my favourite spots in Rome is the courtyard of the Palazzo Spada, with its fragrant orange trees. On one side, you see a long colonnade, at the far end of which stands a life-size statue of a Roman warrior. But it's a deception, a misleadingly life-like use of forced perspective created by the Baroque architect Borromini.
In the *trompe l'œil* style, a layer of crispy potatoes represents the scales of the fish in this dish. Here, nothing is as it seems. Have another look, and prepare your taste buds for an adventure.

Preparation time: 10 minutes plus marinating and soaking

Cooking time: 35 minutes

Serves 2

125ml (4fl oz) dry white wine

sprig of thyme, finely chopped

1 bay leaf, finely chopped

1/2 teaspoon chopped rosemary leaves

3 tablespoons chopped curly parsley leaves

3 tablespoons extra virgin olive oil, plus extra for greasing and drizzling

1 x 600-g (1lb 5-oz) sea bream or sea bass, cleaned, gutted and scaled (ask your fishmonger to do this for you)

1kg (2lb 4oz) medium floury potatoes, such as Maris Piper

35g (1¼oz) unsalted butter, melted

salt and pepper

In a small bowl, stir together the wine, chopped herbs and olive oil and season with salt and pepper. Place the sea bream in a large dish and brush inside and out with the herby marinade to ensure it is evenly coated. Transfer to the refrigerator and leave to marinate for 30 minutes.

Meanwhile, peel, wash and dry the potatoes before cutting them into 5-mm (1/4-inch) slices. Drop the potato slices into a bowl filled with water and leave them to rest for 10 minutes to release any excess starch.

Drain the potatoes, then drop them into a saucepan of salted boiling water and blanch for 8–10 minutes. Drain again and leave to cool on baking paper.

Preheat the oven to 180°C (350°F), Gas Mark 4. Line an oven tray with baking paper and grease with a little olive oil.

Arrange half the potatoes on the prepared oven tray to form a silhouette as long and as wide as the sea bream itself, season them with salt and pepper and drizzle over a little extra oil.

Remove the fish from the marinade and place it on top of the potato layer, then arrange the remaining potatoes over the fish in an overlapping pattern as if they were scales. Brush everything with olive oil and season with salt and pepper.

Cover the head and tail of the fish with aluminium foil, spoon over three-quarters of the marinade and bake for 10 minutes, then lower the heat to 160°C (325°F), Gas Mark 3 and bake for a further 10 minutes, until the fish is almost cooked through. Turn the grill on to high, brush the fish with melted butter and cook for a final 5 minutes until golden.

Remove the fish from the oven and transfer to a serving plate. Serve warm, with the remaining marinade in a small bowl on the side as a sauce.

Costolette d'agnello in crosta con cavolfiore e castagne accompagnate
da gattò di patate, cardi e arance

CRISPY LAMB CUTLETS WITH CAULIFLOWER & CHESTNUTS ACCOMPANIED BY A POTATO & ORANGE SAVOURY CAKE

Goethe once said 'see Naples and die'. I like to think something like 'see Rome and live better, in a fuller, more aware way, with history and personal memories running side by side, making this city your own'. The city's food also speaks directly to the heart with a sense of simplicity – of living in the present moment – that is reflected in this flavoursome dish. If you can't find cardoons to make the savoury cake here, you can use celery, chard stems or artichoke instead.

Preparation time: 20 minutes plus resting

Cooking time: 1 hour

Serves 2

100g (3½oz) plain flour, plus extra for dusting

50g (1¾oz) ground almonds

60g (2¼oz) cold unsalted butter, cut into 1-cm (½-inch) cubes

1 teaspoon salt

1 teaspoon cold water

150g (5½oz) cauliflower, trimmed and cut into 1-cm (½-inch) chunks

3 tablespoons extra virgin olive oil

1 garlic clove, peeled and left whole

30g (1oz) whole cooked chestnuts, cut into 1-cm (½-inch) chunks

4 lamb loin cutlets

1 egg yolk mixed together with 1 tablespoon milk, to glaze

50g (1¾oz) flaked almonds

Potato and orange savoury cake:

100g (3½oz) cardoons, trimmed and cut into 10-cm (4-inch) lengths

In a food processor, blend together the flour, ground almonds, butter, salt and cold water for a few seconds until combined. Transfer to a flat surface and quickly bring the ingredients together with your fingertips to form a flaky dough. You don't want to overwork it, or you'll end up with soggy pastry. Wrap in clingfilm and leave to rest in the refrigerator for 30 minutes.

Meanwhile, bring a large saucepan of salted water to a boil, add the cauliflower pieces and blanch for 8 minutes until tender. Drain well and dry on a clean tea towel.

Heat the oil in a frying pan over a medium heat, add the garlic and cook, stirring, for 5 minutes until golden. Remove the garlic from the pan, add the cauliflower and chestnuts and cook for 5 minutes, until crispy and lightly golden, then remove them from the pan and set aside. Lower the lamb cutlets into the pan and brown for 1 minute on each side. Set aside to cool, then pat dry with kitchen paper.

For the potato and orange savoury cake, bring a saucepan of salted water to a boil, add the cardoon and potato chunks and cook for 15 minutes, then add the potato slices and cook for a further 5 minutes. Drain well and dry on kitchen paper, setting the sliced potatoes aside.

Pass the potato chunks through a potato ricer into a bowl, then add the egg, parsley, nutmeg, milk, orange juice, cardoons and half of the butter and Parmesan. Season with salt and mix together until smooth.

Brush the surface of a 15-cm (6-inch) oven dish or individual small ramekins with the oil and scatter over half the breadcrumbs. Spoon over half the mashed potato mixture, place the ham and cheese strips on top and finish with the remaining mashed potato. Spread the potato slices over the surface, scatter over the rest of the Parmesan cheese and breadcrumbs and dot with the remaining butter. Set aside.

300g (10½oz) potatoes, cut into
2-cm (¾-inch) chunks, plus
2 extra, thinly sliced, to decorate

1 large egg

handful of flat-leaf parsley leaves,
very finely chopped

1 teaspoon ground nutmeg

50ml (2fl oz) milk

zest and juice of 1 orange

40g (1½oz) unsalted butter

35g (1¼oz) Parmesan cheese,
grated

2 tablespoons extra virgin olive oil

50g (1¾oz) breadcrumbs (*see*
page 262)

30g (1oz) roast ham, thinly sliced
and cut into 1-cm (½-inch)
strips

50g (1¾oz) provolone cheese,
thinly sliced and cut into 1-cm
(½-inch) strips

salt

Preheat the oven to 200°C (400°F), Gas Mark 6.

Roll the chilled pastry out on a clean floured surface to a thickness of 5mm
(¼ inch) and cut it into four rectangles large enough to cover the cutlets,
each about 5cm (2 inches) x 10cm (4 inches) in size. Place a meat cutlet in
the middle of a pastry piece, cover with a tablespoon of the cauliflower and
chestnut mixture and wrap the edges over to seal tightly in place like a
parcel, leaving the rib bone outside the pastry. Repeat with the remaining
cutlets, then brush each pastry 'parcel' with the egg and milk glaze and
sprinkle over the flaked almonds. Wrap the cutlet bones in aluminium foil
to finish, to prevent them from burning in the oven.

Put the potato cake into the oven and cook for 5 minutes, then add the
lamb cutlets and cook for 20–25 minutes, until the pastry on the cutlets
is golden.

Remove the cutlets from the oven and set aside, then turn the grill to high
and cook the potato cake for 10 minutes more until crispy and golden.
Remove the potato cake from the oven, sprinkle over the orange zest and
remaining parsley and serve alongside the lamb cutlets.

Ravioli alla Romana con broccoli, alici, pomodori secchi e ricotta

ROMAN-STYLE RAVIOLI WITH BROCCOLI, ANCHOVIES, SUN-DRIED TOMATOES & RICOTTA

A ray of sunlight hits my favourite spot in the Biblioteca Angelica as I get lost in a book. Looking at the endless bookshelves, browsing through the card index, respecting the rule of silence – everything about this place is life-enhancing. As I leave the library, thinking that my day couldn't get any better, I see a *pastificio*. Making pasta by hand always makes me feel good. I like to experiment, so here basil-flavoured pasta meets a filling of ricotta, sun-dried tomatoes and anchovies. Free your imagination, lose yourself in eternity.

Preparation time: 30 minutes

Cooking time: 25 minutes

Serves 2

100g (3½oz) plain flour

1 egg, beaten

10 basil leaves, chopped, plus extra to serve

pinch of salt

70g (2½oz) Parmesan or ricotta salata cheese, grated

Filling:

4 anchovies in olive oil, drained

120g (4½oz) ricotta cheese

10 sun-dried tomatoes

Sauce:

2 tablespoons extra virgin olive oil

2 anchovies in olive oil, drained

200g (7oz) purple broccoli, roughly chopped

pinch of chilli flakes

150ml (¼ pint) vegetable stock

50g (1¾oz) walnut pieces

For the filling, put all the ingredients in a food processor and blend together until well combined. Cover and refrigerate until needed.

For the sauce, gently heat the olive oil and the anchovies together in a frying pan over a medium heat for 5 minutes, stirring occasionally, until the anchovies have dissolved. Add the broccoli pieces to the pan together with the chilli flakes, stock and half the walnut pieces, bring to a simmer and cook for 15 minutes, until the broccoli pieces are tender and the liquid has reduced by a third.

Meanwhile, make the egg pasta dough. Place the flour on a large board or a clean, floured work surface. Make a well in the centre and put the beaten egg, chopped basil leaves and salt in it.

Using the tips of your fingers, mix the eggs with the flour, incorporating a little at a time, until everything is combined. Knead the pieces of dough together until you have one big, smooth lump of dough, then divide it into two pieces.

Using a rolling pin, roll one dough portion out to a 2-mm (1/16-inch) thickness and into a 35-cm (14-inch) x 23-cm (9-inch) rectangle. Working quickly, place teaspoonfuls of filling 2.5cm (1 inch) apart over one half of the pasta sheet and brush lightly around the filling with water to moisten. Fold the sheet over and press down around the fillings to seal, then cut out the ravioli squares around the filling using a pastry wheel. Repeat with the remaining dough and filling.

Bring a large saucepan of salted water to a boil, add the ravioli and cook for 3 minutes, or until they float to the surface. As the ravioli are ready, scoop them up with a slotted spoon and transfer them to a large bowl along with half the broccoli sauce and a ladleful of the pasta cooking water. Once you have fished out all the ravioli, add the rest of the sauce, sprinkle over the grated Parmesan, remaining walnuts and a few extra basil leaves and serve.

Spiedini di anguille in foglie di alloro e salsa al cren

EEL & BAY LEAF SKEWERS WITH HOMEMADE HORSERADISH SAUCE

In the days of the Roman Empire, a victorious military commander was crowned with a laurel wreath. An officer would recite the *memento mori* – bear in mind that one day you will die – to remind him that glory was only temporary. *Abbassa la cresta*, you'd better lower your crest, as we would say today to those who think too highly of themselves.
It's worth trying to find fresh horseradish root for this recipe – try ethnic greengrocers or a farmers' market – but you can always buy ready-made horseradish sauce.

Preparation time: 15 minutes plus marinating

Cooking time: 10–15 minutes

Serves 2

400g (14oz) fresh eels, skinned, gutted, boned and cut into 5-cm (2-inch) logs (ask your fishmonger to do this for you)

6 tablespoons extra virgin olive oil

1 garlic clove, peeled and left whole

375ml (13fl oz) dry white wine

10 black peppercorns

12 bay leaves

large handful of finely chopped curly parsley leaves

Sauce:

4 tablespoons freshly grated horseradish

1 tablespoon white wine vinegar

1 teaspoon caster sugar

1 tablespoon extra virgin olive oil

1 tablespoon breadcrumbs (*see* page 262)

Combine the eel pieces in a large food bag with the oil, garlic, wine and peppercorns. Shake well and leave to marinate in the refrigerator for 2 hours.

While the eel is marinating, soak six bamboo skewers in water (this will prevent them from burning during cooking).

Preheat the grill to high.

Remove the eel pieces from the marinade, reserving the liquid. Alternately thread two pieces of fish and two bay leaves onto each skewer and brush each with the marinade. Lay the skewers on the centre rack of the oven and grill for 10–15 minutes, turning and brushing the eel with the marinade halfway through cooking, until the eel pieces are charred and cooked through.

Meanwhile, prepare the sauce by mixing the grated horseradish, vinegar, sugar, oil and breadcrumbs together in a bowl until well combined.

Arrange the skewers on plates, scatter over the chopped parsley and serve alongside the creamed horseradish sauce and a Puntarelle Salad (*see* page 120), if you like.

Penne gratinate alla Campolattaro

CAMPOLATTARO-STYLE PENNE GRATIN

Mirror, mirror on the wall, who is the fairest of them all? I love how simple ingredients can turn into something spectacular. It's the 29th of June. Outside, choirs and street bands celebrate the Feast of St Peter and St Paul, observed in Rome as a public holiday. Indoors, there is the aroma of enchanting creaminess. Simmer, poach, fry. Soften, sift, emulsify. Comforting gestures to help get the most out of everyday life. Keeping it light while making a desirable pasta dish. Staying in is the new going out.

Preparation time: 10 minutes

Cooking time: 45 minutes

Serves 2

2 tablespoons extra virgin olive oil

1 x 100-g (3½-oz) chicken breast, cut into 1-cm (½-inch) slices

15g (½oz) black truffle, finely sliced

50g (1¾oz) prosciutto, finely sliced

2 tablespoons Cognac

5 tablespoons double cream

100g (3½oz) Parmesan cheese, grated

150g (5½oz) penne rigate pasta

50g (1¾oz) breadcrumbs (*see* page 262)

25g (1oz) unsalted butter, cut into 5-mm (¼-inch) cubes

salt and pepper

Heat the oil in a small non-stick frying pan over a medium heat, add the chicken pieces and cook, stirring, for 5–7 minutes, until the chicken is lightly browned and cooked through. Add the truffle, prosciutto and Cognac to the pan, bring to a simmer and cook for 5 minutes until the liquid has evaporated. Stir in the cream and half the Parmesan and remove from the heat.

Tip half of the sauce into a food processor and blend until smooth. Return to the pan and stir everything together well.

Preheat the oven to 180°C (350°F), Gas Mark 4.

Bring a saucepan of salted water to a boil, add the penne and cook for half the time suggested on the packet, then drain the pasta and tip it into a small baking dish. Add the sauce, season with salt and pepper and mix well. Sprinkle over the breadcrumbs and remaining Parmesan and dot with the butter.

Bake the penne gratin for 30 minutes until the crust is golden and crisp. Leave to rest for 10 minutes before serving with a green salad.

Seppioline piselli, avocado e pomodoro

SQUID WITH PEAS, AVOCADO & TOMATOES

This piquantly spicy dish facilitates the best conversations, the kind you normally wouldn't even dream of having without it as a go-between. That's the miracle of partaking of a meal together: there's a solemn sense of ceremony and people are at once very eager to listen and thrilled to speak, their intentions heightened by sharing an intimate moment. Life may be a pantomime, but dinner... that's serious stuff.

Preparation time: 15 minutes plus marinating

Cooking time: 1 hour 25 minutes

Serves 4 for a double date

1kg (2lb 4oz) squid or baby squid, cleaned and tentacles separated (ask the fishmonger to do this for you)

3 tablespoons extra virgin olive oil

juice of 1 lemon

small handful of curly parsley leaves, very finely chopped

small handful of coriander leaves, very finely chopped

1 red onion, finely chopped

1 garlic clove

1 celery stick, trimmed and finely chopped

100ml (3½fl oz) dry white wine

300g (10½oz) cherry tomatoes, halved

350g (12oz) garden peas, defrosted if frozen

500ml (18fl oz) vegetable stock

1 avocado, stone removed and cut into 1-cm (½-inch) cubes

½ teaspoon Tabasco sauce

salt

Take a squid tube and place a large chef's knife flat inside it. Using a second knife, slice the squid three times on each side, as if you're cutting it into rings (you won't be able to cut all the way because of the other knife).

Place the prepared squid tubes along with the tentacles in a sealable food bag with half the olive oil, lemon juice, parsley and coriander. Transfer to the refrigerator and leave to marinate for 2 hours.

When ready to cook, heat the rest of the oil in a large non-stick frying pan over a low heat, add the onion, garlic and celery and cook, stirring, for 10 minutes, until soft and translucent. Remove the squid from the marinade and add it to the pan together with the wine and tomatoes. Increase the heat to high, bring to a vigorous simmer and cook, stirring, for 15 minutes, until all the liquid has evaporated.

Reduce the heat to low, season with salt and add the peas and stock to the pan. Simmer very gently, stirring occasionally, for 45 minutes, then stir in the avocado pieces and the remaining lemon juice and cook for a further 15 minutes, until the sauce is thick and the squid is tender.

Remove the squid from the heat and leave to cool slightly, before stirring in the Tabasco sauce. Scatter over the rest of the fresh herbs and serve with a dry white wine such as Soave or Pinot Grigio.

Any leftovers can be kept in the refrigerator for up to 3 days.

Chapter 7 #FOODHAPPINESS SUPPERS

Italy is sometimes known as the land of Cockaigne, an ideal place where prosperity, abundance and gratification are available to everyone. It's easy to believe – just keep your eyes closed and dream on.

There is a powerful magic among people sharing a meal. Personal anecdotes mix and whirl audaciously while diners relish their pasta. Perhaps it's because they find themselves repeating a ritual linked to the history of the dish itself. I myself always feel the need to understand the origins of what I'm biting into, and that's why at my table, I strive for authenticity and time-honoured tradition. There's an honesty about eating together, and it is without a doubt one of the most straightforward ways of appreciating our relationships with those we love. Everyone is more like themselves at the dining table. We eat together when we want to spend quality time in someone's company.

Sharing food is not simply about that almost inevitable stain on the tablecloth after enjoying a good Pollo alla Romana (*see* page 179). Crucially, it leaves us intensely exposed to others. Often this happens without us even noticing, but I believe it doesn't go unnoticed by our soul. The more the ingredients respond to the truest nature of the dish, the more we are bound to have a heartfelt experience. And that's what #foodhappiness is all about: it's that grin on people's faces, their eager anticipation when they're presented with a dish full of promise. It's that reflective pause, the overwhelming contemplation, the thrilled expectation – #foodhappiness brings out the best in everyone.

It's also linked to art, but please don't mistake this with some chef's habit of putting big food in small dishes. No, it's another art I refer to: the winning skill of *arrangiarsi*, of making do – producing a miraculous dish using only three ingredients or transforming leftovers into something even more delicious. Back in the 1970s, a group of Italian painters including Mario Schifano and Renato Guttuso used to draw on the paper tablecloths of the Roman trattoria they used as their personal canteen. In return for these sketches, they would get a plate of pasta, a bottle of wine and the host's eternal gratitude for having boosted the standing of his restaurant. Old recipes, new meanings. A blast from the past carrying contemporary values.

Pollo alla Romana con peperoni

ROMAN-STYLE CHICKEN WITH PEPPERS

Sora Lella used to go to the Campo dei Fiori market every single day. Even if the grocer told her *'È speciale!'* she would taste each ingredient and, if satisfied, buy a whole case. Back at her restaurant, on the Isola Tiberina, she made classic Roman dishes: 'I beg of you, when in Rome, the only way to have your chicken is Roman style!' What's special about this dish is the sweet and sour taste of the peppers melting into the chicken. My own twist on this dish is the addition of pungent black olives and some flaked almonds scattered on top. A spellbinding crunchy delight for an unforgettable bite.

Preparation time: 10 minutes

Cooking time: 45 minutes

Serves 6

4 tablespoons extra virgin olive oil

1 large white onion, finely chopped

1 x 2-kg (4-lb 8-oz) free-range chicken, jointed, or the equivalent amount of chicken pieces

120ml (4fl oz) white wine

500g (1lb 2oz) baby plum or large vine tomatoes, finely chopped

1 large red pepper, cored, deseeded and cut into thin strips

1 large green pepper, cored, deseeded and cut into thin strips

1 large yellow pepper, cored, deseeded and cut into thin strips

80g (3oz) black pitted olives

handful of basil leaves

50g (1³/₄oz) flaked almonds

salt and pepper

Heat half the oil and onion in a saucepan over a medium heat for 3–4 minutes, until the onion has softened and browned.

Add the chicken pieces to the pan and season with a little salt and pepper. Cook, stirring occasionally, for 10 minutes, until the chicken is lightly browned on all sides. Pour over the wine, bring to a vigorous simmer and let it evaporate, then add half the tomatoes and reduce the heat to low. Leave to simmer gently for 30 minutes, until the chicken pieces are tender and cooked through (you can judge this by cutting into the largest pieces with a knife – if the centre is no longer pink, the chicken is ready).

Meanwhile, heat the remaining oil and onion in a separate saucepan until the onion has browned. Add the peppers and cook for 5 minutes, stirring, until softened, then add the olives, basil and the rest of the tomatoes. Simmer gently for 30 minutes while the chicken is cooking.

Remove both the chicken and pepper mixtures from the heat and combine the two together. Leave to cool slightly before serving sprinkled with flaked almonds.

Pasta cacio, pepe e cozze

PASTA WITH CHEESE, PEPPER & MUSSELS

As much as I love seafood, I used to be put off by the idea of cleaning mussels myself, but it's really not that hard. The rope-grown mussels you find in good supermarkets are fairly clean already, so just rinse them under cold running water, then remove any remaining 'beards', as those stringy threads that cling to the outside of the shell are known. If you come across a stubborn one, take hold of it with dry kitchen paper and pull it downwards until it comes out. If you find a wide-open mussel in your batch, check if it's still alive by tapping it against another mussel, *tlack tlack tlack*. The mussel should gradually close up. If it doesn't, you've got a dead one on your hands. Toss it and move on: it's time to make that creamy sauce now.

Preparation time: 20 minutes

Cooking time: 15 minutes

Serves 4

3 tablespoons extra virgin olive oil

1 garlic clove, peeled and left whole

large handful of flat-leaf parsley leaves, finely chopped

handful of dill, finely chopped

700g (1lb 9oz) rope-grown mussels, cleaned and de-bearded (see above)

400g (14oz) farfalle or pappardelle pasta

150g (5½oz) pecorino romano cheese, very finely grated

100g (3½oz) roasted peanuts

salt and pepper

Heat 2 tablespoons of olive oil in a non-stick frying pan over a low heat, add the garlic and cook for 2–3 minutes until lightly browned.

Add half the chopped parsley and dill to the pan along with the mussels. Increase the heat to medium, cover with a lid and cook for 5 minutes, until the mussels have opened fully.

Tip the mussels into a colander set above a bowl. Discard any that haven't opened and reserve the mussel cooking liquid that gathers in the bowl. You can extract the mussel meat and discard the shells, if you prefer, or leave the mussels in their shells.

Bring a large saucepan of lightly salted water to a boil, add the pasta and cook according to the packet instructions until a few minutes before al dente.

While the pasta is cooking, mix together the grated pecorino with a ladleful or so of the pasta cooking water and whizz everything together with a hand-held blender to form a creamy sauce. Season with pepper and set aside. Heat the remaining tablespoon of olive oil in a saucepan over a medium heat, add the mussel cooking liquid and simmer for 1 minute until slightly thickened and reduced.

Drain the cooked pasta, reserving four ladlefuls of the pasta cooking water, and transfer it to the saucepan with the mussel cooking liquid. Add the cooked mussels, pecorino sauce and peanuts and sprinkle over the remaining herbs. Gradually add the pasta water, stirring, until the sauce is thick and creamy. Season generously with pepper and serve.

Braciole di maiale con panuntelle

PORK CHOPS WITH GREASED BREAD

Preparation time: 10 minutes plus marinating

Cooking time: 40 minutes

Serves 6

6 pork chops

6 tablespoons extra virgin olive oil

3 garlic cloves, peeled and left whole

small handful of rosemary leaves, plus extra sprigs to garnish

2 tablespoons lemon juice

375ml (13fl oz) dry white wine

15 black peppercorns

4 juniper berries

6 slices of rustic bread

2 cucumbers, trimmed and thinly sliced

salt and pepper

Salad:

250g (9oz) parsnips, peeled and cut into wedges

250g (9oz) baby beetroot, peeled and cut into wedges

2 Bramley or other cooking apples, peeled, cored and cut into wedges

1 tablespoon extra virgin olive oil

Dressing:

150ml (¼ pint) natural yogurt

1 tablespoon white wine vinegar

juice of ½ lemon

small handful of dill fronds

2 tablespoons extra virgin olive oil

This is a humble yet intensely flavoured pork chop recipe. *Panuntella* means greased bread: place your pork chops (with a nice ring of fat around them) on a grill rack over slices of good rustic bread and let the drippings transform it as the pork gently cooks. Serve with a colourful wintery salad, made all the more desirable by its freshness. Embark on a wonderful food affair.

Place the pork chops in a large food bag with the oil, garlic, rosemary, lemon juice, wine, peppercorns and juniper berries. Seal and shake to mix everything together well, then transfer to the refrigerator and leave to marinate for 1 hour.

Preheat the oven to 200°C (400°F), Gas Mark 6.

While the pork chops are marinating, prepare the salad. Arrange the parsnip, beetroot and apple wedges in a large roasting tin, drizzle over the olive oil and bake in the oven for 25 minutes, turning halfway during cooking, until softened. Remove from the oven, season with salt and pepper and leave to cool.

Switch the oven setting to a high grill.

For the dressing, mix all the ingredients together in a small bowl. Season with salt and pepper.

Remove the pork chops from the marinade and place them on an oven rack under the hot grill, arranging the pieces of bread in an ovenproof dish directly below the chops to catch all the delicious cooking juices. Cook for 15 minutes, turning the chops halfway, until golden and cooked through.

Remove the chops and bread slices from the oven. Cover the bread with the cucumber slices, then arrange the pork chops on top and finish each piece with a sprig of rosemary. Season with salt and pepper. Toss the salad in the dressing to coat and serve alongside the chops and bread.

Tesoro di riso e sogliole con salsa al prosecco

RICE & LEMON SOLE TIMBALE
WITH PROSECCO GRAVY

Here is a flamboyant dish that will capture everyone's attention – the wow factor is assured.
This dish encapsulates #foodhappiness at its best. With a *timballo*, any night is a big night.
Ask your fishmonger to save the bones when preparing the sole fillets, as they will make
a good addition to the stock.

Preparation time: 10 minutes

Cooking time: 1¼ hours

Serves 10

olive oil, for greasing

100g (3½oz) unsalted butter

1 shallot, finely sliced

700g (1lb 9oz) carnaroli or arborio
    risotto rice

200g (7oz) Parmesan cheese,
    grated

½ teaspoon white pepper

100g (3½oz) plain flour

1 teaspoon ground nutmeg

300ml (½ pint) single cream

500ml (18fl oz) prosecco

7 x 100-g (3½-oz) lemon sole
    fillets, deboned and skinned
    (ask your fishmonger to do this
    for you)

zest of 1 orange, cut into thin
    matchsticks

zest of 1 lemon, cut into thin
    matchsticks

salt and pepper

Stock:

3 litres (5¼ pints) water

1 carrot

1 celery stick, trimmed

1 large white onion

handful of curly parsley leaves

salt

For the stock, pour the measured water into a large saucepan and add the carrot, celery, onion and parsley along with any fish bones you may have reserved from the sole. Season generously with salt and simmer over a medium heat for 30 minutes or so, until the stock has reduced by a third. Keep warm over a low heat.

Preheat the oven to 200°C (400°F), Gas Mark 6. Grease a non-stick 25-cm (10-inch) fluted ring cake tin with a drizzle of olive oil.

Melt a knob of butter in a heavy-based saucepan, add the shallot and cook over a medium heat for 10 minutes until soft. Add the rice and cook, stirring, for 2–3 minutes until translucent, then add a ladleful of the hot stock. Season generously with salt and continue to cook over a medium heat, stirring, until all the stock has been absorbed. Keep adding ladlefuls of stock, stirring constantly, allowing each ladleful to be absorbed before adding the next, until the rice no longer has a pale core and is soft but still retains a slight bite. This will take around 15 minutes.

Remove the risotto from the heat and add the Parmesan, pepper and a knob of butter. Set aside.

In a separate small saucepan, melt the remaining butter and whisk in the flour to form a paste (roux). Stirring all the while, slowly add the nutmeg, cream, prosecco and enough fish stock to make a smooth, pale gravy. Simmer gently for 5 minutes over a low heat to thicken slightly, then remove from the heat and set aside.

Press the sole fillets against the bottom and sides of the prepared cake tin to line it, leaving the fillets overhanging slightly at the top. Season well with salt and pepper. Spoon the risotto into the mould, pressing it down with the back of a spoon to pack it as tightly as possible, then pour over half the prosecco gravy. Carefully transfer the tin to the oven and bake for 15–20 minutes until lightly golden and set.

Remove from the oven and leave to rest for 30 minutes before carefully turning out onto a large serving dish. Scatter over the zest strips and serve with the remaining gravy.

Porchetta di Ariccia e cavoli trascinati

ARICCIA-STYLE ROAST PORK WITH 'DRAGGED' SAVOY CABBAGE

In Rome, people of all kinds mix in an almost contradictory way: you see the vagabond with the prince, the lawyer with the butcher, the florist with that mysterious lady always dressed in black. It might be due to the sweet air, or the typical disposition of the native Romans, who are hardly shocked by anything, ever. Just look at the way most of them walk – *trascinati*, almost as if dragged along by an invisible force, a form of vigorous sloth.

Porchetta is one of those dishes that tastes even better a couple of days after it has been made. It can be served in slices as a main course, but in Rome it is usually consumed in a sandwich bought from a street vendor. After testing this recipe numerous times – and ending up with a smelly oven and smellier hair – I finally found a way to achieve the ultimate pleasure of this dish while keeping the oven in a decent state and my mascara intact.

About the cabbage: I know this sounds like a British side dish but it is, as we Italians say, *per davvero*, no joke. I love cabbage, and the combination with the loveliest melting pork really makes my heart sing. *Porchetta* and cabbage – a love affair of guilty pleasures.

Preparation time: 30 minutes

Cooking time: 2½ hours

Serves 10

1 x 1.3-kg (3-lb) boned pork belly, rind left on

small handful of rosemary leaves

large handful of sage leaves, chopped

2 teaspoons dried oregano

1 tablespoon fennel seeds

2 teaspoons ground nutmeg

1 x 2-kg (4lb 8-oz) boneless pork loin

5 tablespoons extra virgin olive oil

salt and pepper

Place the pork belly skin-side up on a board. Holding the blade of a sharp knife parallel to the board, cut along the length of the belly but not all the way through. Unfold the belly so that it opens like a book, then rub over a third of the herbs and spices and season generously with salt and pepper.

Place the pork loin in the middle of the belly, season with salt and pepper and rub over another third of the herbs and spices. Roll the pork belly around the loin into a cylindrical shape and tie everything firmly together with kitchen string. Using a very sharp knife, score the skin in a diagonal pattern, then wrap everything with aluminium foil before tying it firmly with kitchen string once more.

Bring a large casserole dish of salted water to a boil. Reduce the heat to a simmer, lower the *porchetta* into the water and leave to cook over a low-medium heat, covered, for 1 hour, then carefully remove the *porchetta* from the water and leave to cool for 10–15 minutes.

Coat the bottom of a large baking dish with the olive oil and remaining herbs and spices. Preheat the oven to 200°C (400°F), Gas Mark 6.

Once the *porchetta* is cool, remove the aluminium foil. Place it in the prepared baking dish and roast for 1 hour until the skin is crispy and golden. Remove from the oven and leave to cool for 30 minutes.

Cabbage:

1 whole Savoy cabbage, trimmed

10 small new potatoes

100ml (3½fl oz) extra virgin olive oil

2 garlic cloves, peeled and left whole

3 white rustic bread slices, cut into 1-cm (½-inch) cubes

salt

While the *porchetta* is cooling, make the cabbage. Remove ten large external leaves from the cabbage (these will serve as shells for the dish itself) and roughly cut the remainder into 2-cm (¾-inch) chunks.

Bring a large pot of salted water to a boil. Add the potatoes and cook for 5 minutes, then add the cabbage pieces and leaves to the pan and boil for a further 5 minutes. Drain and let cool.

When the cabbage leaves are cool enough to handle, wring out any excess water with your hands and form the leaves into 10 equal-sized balls. Peel the potatoes and cut them into 5-mm (¼-inch) chunks.

Heat the oil in a large frying pan over a medium heat. Add the garlic cloves and cook, stirring occasionally, for 5 minutes until golden. Remove the garlic from the pan, add the bread cubes and cook for 3 minutes until lightly browned, then add the cabbage balls and the potato chunks and cook over a medium-low heat, stirring gently, for 15 minutes. Season with salt, then remove from the heat.

Arrange a few tablespoons of the cabbage and potato mixture in the centre of the reserved cabbage leaves and serve alongside the *porchetta*, cut into thick slices.

Maccheroni alla Gricia con carciofi, zucchine e ricotta salata

MACCHERONI WITH ARTICHOKES, COURGETTES & RICOTTA SALATA

I nearly collapsed in surprise when I found out that this recipe, which is considered the forerunner of Amatriciana sauce (*see* opposite), is almost 1,000 years old.
In the past, country folks would sell their cheese at the market and keep any leftover ricotta for themselves, letting it dry and adding salt to preserve it for longer. They would then add this *ricotta salata* – which can be found in most Italian delis – to their pasta. This sauce can turn into stringy mush if you're not careful, so make sure to grate the ricotta as finely as possible.

Preparation time: 25 minutes

Cooking time: 35–45 minutes

Serves 6

3 courgettes, finely sliced

100ml (3½fl oz) vegetable oil

3 tablespoons extra virgin olive oil

1 garlic clove, peeled and left whole

handful of mint leaves, finely chopped

5 fresh artichokes, cleaned (*see* page 13) and cut into 1-cm (½-inch slices), or 200g (7oz) canned artichoke hearts

20 black peppercorns

250g (9oz) *guanciale*, cut into 5-mm (¼-inch) cubes

500g (1lb 2oz) calamarata, garganelli or maccheroni pasta

160g (6oz) *ricotta salata dura* or Parmesan cheese, grated

salt

Cut the courgettes into matchsticks and pat dry with kitchen paper to absorb any excess water.

Heat the vegetable oil in a large non-stick frying pan or deep-fryer to 180–190°C (350–375°F) or until a cube of bread dropped into the oil browns in 30 seconds. Carefully lower the courgette pieces into the hot oil and cook for 5–6 minutes until brown and crispy. Remove from the oil, drain on kitchen paper and season with salt. Set aside.

Heat the olive oil in a small saucepan over medium heat, add the garlic, mint and artichokes and cook for 5 minutes (if you're using fresh artichokes, add a ladleful of boiling water and cook for a further 5–10 minutes to ensure the artichoke pieces are tender).

Toast the peppercorns in a small non-stick frying pan for 5 minutes over a medium heat, then roughly crush them with the side of a heavy knife.

Heat a heavy-based frying pan or cast-iron skillet over a medium heat, add the *guanciale* pieces and leave to fry in their own fat, stirring occasionally, for 10 minutes or until crispy.

Bring a large saucepan of salted water to a boil. Add the pasta and cook according to the packet instructions until al dente. Drain, reserving 150ml (¼ pint) of the pasta cooking water.

Transfer the grated *ricotta salata* to a food processor and whiz for about 10 seconds – you want the cheese to be as finely grated as possible. Place the ricotta in a small bowl and mix it together with a ladleful of the reserved pasta cooking water and half the crushed peppercorns until nice and creamy.

Mix together the pasta and the artichoke mixture, then pour over the creamy ricotta sauce. Add a ladleful of the cooking water and stir everything together until the sauce is loose and velvety in texture. To finish, mix in the *guanciale* and serve topped with the deep-fried courgettes and the remaining crushed peppercorns.

Pasta all'Amatriciana

PASTA WITH AMATRICIANA SAUCE

This masterpiece of the Roman kitchen – topped with *guanciale*, cured pork cheek – reminds me of a popular Roman song. Take any *osteria* on the outskirts of the city on a Friday night: a group of Romans of all ages, piping hot pasta all'Amatriciana, a straw-wrapped *fiasco* of wine and a chorus of *La Società dei Magnaccioni* – the Society of Big Eaters:

La società de li magnaccioni, (This is the Big Eaters Society)
La società de la gioventù, (This is the society fit for youth)
A noi ce piace de magnà e beve, (we love to eat and drink)
E nun ce piace de lavorà. (and we don't like to work)

Preparation time: 5 minutes

Cooking time: 35 minutes

Serves 6

250g (9oz) *guanciale*, cut into
    5mm (¼-inch) cubes

2 tablespoons extra virgin olive oil

sprig of thyme

1 small banana shallot, finely sliced

500g (1lb 2oz) peeled plum
    tomatoes

½ teaspoon caster sugar

pinch of chilli flakes

500g (1lb 2oz) bucatini, rigatoni or
    mezze maniche pasta

250g (9oz) pecorino romano
    cheese, grated

salt

Heat a heavy-based frying pan or cast-iron skillet over a medium heat, add the *guanciale* pieces and leave to fry in their own fat, stirring occasionally, for 10 minutes until crispy.

Gently heat the olive oil together with the thyme in a separate large non-stick frying pan. Add the shallot and cook, stirring, for 5 minutes until softened, then add the tomatoes, breaking them up with the back of a wooden spoon. Stir in the sugar and chilli flakes and simmer over a medium-low heat for 15 minutes until the sauce has thickened and reduced and the flavours have come together.

Meanwhile, bring a large saucepan of salted water to a boil. Add the pasta and cook according to the packet instructions until al dente, then drain, reserving a cupful of the pasta cooking water.

Add the cooked pasta to the sauce along with half the *guanciale* and its fat. Mix everything together well, adding a little of the cooking water and the remaining *guanciale* fat as you go, until the pasta sauce is loose and velvety in texture. Transfer to a serving dish, sprinkle over the pecorino and the remaining *guanciale* and serve immediately.

Coniglio brodettato della vendemmia con uva e olive

STEWED RABBIT WITH GRAPES & OLIVES

It's September. Harvest time. Time to taste the *novello* – a light, fruity young wine ready to drink in October – or perhaps the *sincero*, which means candid and makes you tipsy before you know it. As the Ancient Romans put it, *in vino veritas*. A *novello* wine can accompany a simple meal or help me in the kitchen. Roman wine doesn't cost a fortune. I keep a bottle with the oil and vinegar, in easy reach, while I'm cooking. Its origins lie in the Roman countryside, home to the Etruscan civilization: places like Frascati, Tarquinia or Cerveteri, home to the Sarcophagus of the Spouses, an ancient terracotta sarcophagus in the form of a couple lounging at a banquet. In my eyes, it is one of the most democratic celebrations of love. Like the blush of a summer sunset on a vineyard flecked with gold and purple.

Preparation time: 10 minutes

Cooking time: 1 hour

Serves 6

4 tablespoons extra virgin olive oil

1 x 1.5-kg (3lb 5-oz) rabbit, jointed into 8 pieces

1 large white onion, chopped

1 garlic clove, crushed

2 bay leaves, plus extra to garnish

handful of sage leaves, roughly chopped

120ml (4fl oz) young red wine

150g (5½fl oz) pitted black olives

approx. 250ml (9fl oz) vegetable stock

100g (3½oz) red grapes

60g (2¼oz) wild rocket leaves, plus extra to garnish

salt and pepper

Heat the oil in a large, heavy-based saucepan over a low heat. Add the rabbit pieces and cook for 10 minutes, turning halfway through cooking, until lightly golden all over.

Add the onion, garlic, bay leaves and sage to the pan and season with salt and pepper. Cook, stirring, for 10 minutes until the onion has softened, then pour over the wine, add the olives and bring to a simmer. Cook uncovered over a low heat for 30–35 minutes, stirring occasionally and adding a ladleful of stock whenever the stew looks in danger of drying out.

Stir the grapes and rocket leaves into the stew and cook for a final 10 minutes, until the stew is thick and glossy and the rabbit meat is falling from the bone.

To serve, scatter a handful of rocket leaves onto an oval serving dish. Spoon over the stew and top with a few extra rocket leaves. Decorate one end of the serving dish with the bay leaves, giving your rabbit stew a 'crown'. Serve with a simple green salad and plenty of bread for mopping up the sauce.

Ribollita Laziale

LAZIO-STYLE RIBOLLITA SOUP

This soup – the perfect example of *cucina povera* – was originally made using up leftover vegetables. With the addition of crunchy water chestnuts, my *ribollita* challenges the norm. It does take a while to prepare but it's stress-free. To give your soup extra depth, ask your butcher for some beef bones or pork rind to add to the beans. Wash, chop and chuck everything into a pot: preparing this soup has a meditative quality. It's not your average soup.

Preparation time: 20 minutes plus overnight soaking

Cooking time: 2 hours

Serves 8

250g (9oz) dried haricot beans

1 teaspoon bicarbonate of soda

2 litres (3½ pints) water

1 x approx. 500-g (1lb 2-oz) beef shank bone or pork rind (optional)

1 large carrot

1 large white onion

1 celery stick, trimmed

1 leek, trimmed and cleaned

250g (9oz) kale, trimmed

250g (9oz) cauliflower, stalk removed

2 large Charlotte potatoes

200g (7oz) Swiss chard, trimmed

250g (9oz) Savoy cabbage, trimmed

250g (9oz) cavolo nero, trimmed

4 tablespoons extra virgin olive oil

150g (5½oz) canned peeled tomatoes

small handful of fresh mixed herbs (thyme, rosemary, sage and bay leaves), tied together with string

200g (7oz) whole water chestnuts, roughly chopped

200g (7oz) rustic bread, cut into 8 slices

salt and pepper

Place the haricot beans in a large bowl, add the bicarbonate of soda and cover with water. Leave to soak overnight.

When ready to cook, drain the soaked beans well. Pour the measured water into a large casserole dish or stockpot and bring to a boil. Add the haricot beans and beef bone or pork rind, if using, and cook, covered, for 1 hour. Remove the beans from the pan using a slotted spoon and reserve the cooking liquid.

Finely chop all the vegetables either by hand or, to save time, in batches in the food processor.

Heat the oil in a large casserole dish over a low heat, add the chopped carrot, onion, celery and leek and cook, stirring, for 10 minutes until the vegetables are softened and translucent. Add the tomatoes and fresh herb bundle along with the rest of the chopped vegetables and half the bean cooking liquid. Bring to a boil, then reduce the heat to a simmer and leave to cook gently for 50 minutes, adding the chopped water chestnuts halfway through cooking.

Tip half the beans into a food processor and blend to a smooth purée. Add the puréed beans to the soup along with the whole beans, season to taste and remove from the heat. Season with salt and pepper.

Remove and discard the herb bundle from the soup. Pour half the soup into the food processor and blend until smooth, then add to the remainder and mix together well.

Line each soup bowl with a piece of bread and ladle over the *ribollita* to serve.

Chapter 8 FESTIVITIES

After the Second World War, Hollywood came to Rome, moving its sets to the Cinecittà film studios. The city was populated by glamorous movie stars, famous directors and pipe-smoking producers, who rented magnificent villas on the Via Appia Antica. It was a splendid time.

In the 1963 movie *Yesterday, Today and Tomorrow*, directed by Vittorio De Sica, Sophia Loren plays Mara, a woman who lives in a charming apartment overlooking Piazza Navona, where she also pursues her profession – the oldest in the world. Her favourite client is Augusto, played by Marcello Mastroianni. Her neighbours regard her with suspicion, but their grandson Umberto, who is studying to become a priest, is on the verge of abandoning his vocation for her. His grandmother wants Mara to discourage him. Mara makes a vow: in return for Umberto returning to the seminary, she will not indulge in any worldly pleasures for one week. Every cloud has a silver lining.

In Italy, every occasion is worthy of a celebration. New Year's Day comes wrapped with the hopes of winning the lottery and a *cotechino* wrapped in pastry (*see* page 218); on the 6th of January, Epiphany brings stockings filled with sweets to reward children who have been good and lumps of 'coal' in the form of crystallized sugar to sweetly punish the bad ones. Women are celebrated on the 8th of March with mimosa cake (*see* page 204). Easter season starts early with a pecorino cheese bread (*see* page 211), when, after the excesses of Carnival and its immoderate intake of *castagnole* (*see* page 223), people are traditionally required to renounce all animal products, the promised rewards being eternal life and an improved waistline. A summer of eating salads is interrupted by Ferragosto, signalling the importance of outdoor togetherness and the pleasures of fruits in syrup (*see* page 217).

December, with its irresistible 'false fish' (*see* page 222), brings with it our desire to be good, or simply a bit better... until the next day, at least. Then there are birthdays, with their endless good wishes, of course. I myself much prefer celebrating unbirthdays, *Alice in Wonderland*-style. I like to find a good excuse for a celebration each and every day, and just be merry. Not for nothing am I utterly and undiplomatically Italian.

Palline ricotta e cocco

RICOTTA & COCONUT BALLS

I use icing sugar for this recipe because it's much easier to combine with the rest of the ingredients, getting the preparation time for this dish down to under 10 minutes. If I were a civilized eater, I would tell you that it takes less time to make these sweet balls of coconut and ricotta than it does to eat them, and that the amount below is enough for about six people. Wait until you try them though – they are so good you will probably want to double the ingredients to satisfy any crowd larger than two.

Preparation time: 10 minutes plus chilling

Makes: about 35 small balls

Serves 2–6 (depending on greed)

300g (10½oz) ricotta cheese

90g (3¼oz) icing sugar

2 tablespoons whipping or single cream

180g (6oz) desiccated coconut, plus extra for dusting

In a large bowl, mix together the ricotta, sugar, cream and two-thirds of the desiccated coconut until soft.

Put the remaining desiccated coconut in a large shallow bowl. Divide the ricotta mixture into small walnut-sized pieces and shape into balls, then roll in the desiccated coconut until evenly coated. Arrange the ricotta balls on a large serving dish, cover with clingfilm and leave to chill in the refrigerator for at least 3 hours before serving.

Mimosa al profumo di ananas con fiorellini zuccherati

PINEAPPLE-FLAVOURED MIMOSA CAKE WITH CANDIED FLOWERS

In the alleys of the eternal city, you might bump into a lady carrying a basket of flowers on her head. 'Would you care for a bunch of violets?' she says, and she offers you a purple bundle as she crosses herself.
On the 8th of March, women are traditionally celebrated with a bunch of mimosa blossoms and a mimosa-shaped cake. Mine is decorated with fresh and candied flowers, which you should make the day before. Be sure to prepare the sponge base in advance, too, as it needs to cool completely before you fill it. This wonderfully fresh dessert makes quite a spectacle.

Preparation time: 45 minutes plus cooling, soaking and overnight drying

Cooking time: 50 minutes

Makes 1 x 23-cm (9-inch) cake

6 eggs

120g (4oz) caster sugar

1 teaspoon ground ginger

1 vanilla pod, split lengthways and seeds scraped

pinch of salt

80g (3oz) cornflour, sifted

80g (3oz) plain flour, sifted

Custard:

3 egg yolks

3 tablespoons caster sugar

360ml (12fl oz) milk

zest of 1 lemon

3 tablespoons plain flour, sifted

100ml (3½fl oz) pineapple juice

Filling:

300ml (10fl oz) whipping cream

50g (1¾oz) icing sugar

300g (10oz) pineapple, trimmed, peeled and cored and cut into 1-cm (½-inch) chunks

For the candied flowers, place the sugar in a small bowl. Coat one of the flowers on all sides with the egg white using a small brush, then hold it over the sugar bowl using a pair of tweezers and gently spoon over the sugar until each petal is coated. Place the flower on a large sheet of baking paper, then repeat with the remaining flowers. Leave to dry at room temperature overnight.

For the sponge cake, preheat the oven to 180°C (350°F), Gas Mark 4. Line a 23-cm (9-inch) spring-form cake tin with baking paper.

Put the eggs, sugar, ginger, vanilla seeds and salt in a bowl and mix together with an electric whisk for 10 minutes until fluffy. Add the sifted flours and whisk for another 1–2 minutes to form a smooth batter.

Pour the batter into the cake tin in an even layer and bake in the centre of the oven for 40 minutes, until the sponge is lightly golden and the centre springs back when pressed lightly with your fingers. Leave the sponge to cool in the tin on a wire rack before turning it out.

While the sponge is cooling, make the pineapple custard. Whisk the egg yolks together with the sugar in a medium saucepan off the heat for 5 minutes until pale and fluffy. Add the milk and lemon zest and heat gently for 2–3 minutes, then stir in the flour and bring to a gentle simmer. Leave the custard to bubble away for a further 2–3 minutes before stirring in the pineapple juice. Continue to simmer, stirring, until the custard is thick enough to coat the back of a spoon, then pour the custard into a bowl and leave to cool for 30 minutes. Cover with clingfilm and transfer to the refrigerator for 2 hours to chill.

For the syrup, put the sugar and water in a small saucepan and bring to a boil. Remove from the heat and stir in the liqueur, then leave to cool at room temperature for 20 minutes.

Syrup:

50g (1¾oz) caster sugar

120ml (4fl oz) water

25ml (1oz) rum, brandy or Cognac

Candied flowers:

50g (1¾oz) caster sugar

25 edible flowers, plus extra fresh
    flower to decorate

1 egg white, beaten

For the filling, pour the cream into a bowl and whisk, adding the icing sugar a tablespoon at a time, until all the sugar is incorporated and the cream is nice and fluffy. Gently fold the whipped cream into the cooled custard together with the pineapple pieces until everything is mixed together well.

To assemble the cake, carefully slice the sponge horizontally a third of the way up into two layers. Set the larger top layer aside, brushing the surface with a little of the syrup to lightly moisten it. With a sharp knife and a spoon, carve out a large circle in the bottom layer almost to the edges of the cake, leaving a depth of 2cm (½ inch) at the bottom. Remove the carved-out sponge from the bottom layer and cut it into 3-mm (⅛-inch) crumb-like cubes. Set aside.

Transfer the hollowed bottom layer to a serving plate. Brush the sides and base generously with the syrup, then fill it with half the pineapple custard. Level the filling off using a spatula, then cover with the larger sponge layer, top-side down.

Brush the top of the cake generously with the soaking syrup, then spread the remaining pineapple custard evenly over the top and sides of the cake, pressing the cake cubes gently into the custard all over to fix them in place. Carefully cover with clingfilm and refrigerate for at least 2 hours until the custard has set firm. Serve cold, decorated with a mixture of fresh and candied edible flowers.

Cuzzupa Pasquale
EASTER BREAD WITH EGGS

This sweet, speckled Easter bread is decorated with an egg, an ancient symbol of rebirth. To shape these breads, find a drawing of a bell online, print it out onto a sheet of A4 paper and cut it out to use as a template, or, if you fancy, purchase a bell-shaped cookie cutter. These edible bell–shaped breads also make a nice Easter table decoration.

Preparation time: 20 minutes

Cooking time: 20 minutes

Makes 4 loaves

2 teaspoons baking powder

6 tablespoons milk

4 eggs

160g (6oz) caster sugar

250g (9oz) plain flour, sifted

250g (9oz) strong white flour, sifted

zest of 1 lemon

100ml (3^1/2fl oz) vegetable oil

To decorate:

5 hard-boiled eggs

100g (3^1/2oz) icing sugar

50ml (2fl oz) milk

50g (1^3/4oz) coloured sugar strands

Preheat the oven to 180°C (350°F), Gas Mark 4. Line a baking tray with baking paper.

Dissolve the baking powder in the milk in a bowl. In a separate bowl, beat the eggs and sugar together until fluffy.

Pour the egg and sugar mixture into a large mixing bowl or the bowl of a stand mixer with the dough hook attachment added. Add the baking powder mixture, flours, lemon zest and vegetable oil and mix together to form a firm dough.

Divide the dough into five equal-sized parts and roll each out on a lightly floured surface into a 10-cm (4-inch) x 20-cm (8-inch) rectangle. Shape the trimmings into four little bells, approximately 1.5cm (^{5}/8 inch) thick and arrange on top of four of the dough rectangles. Place four of the rectangles on the prepared baking sheet and cut the final rectangle across the longest side into eight 1-cm (^{1}/2-inch) wide strips.

To decorate, place an egg in the centre of a bell and lay over two of the dough strips to form a cross over the egg and fix it in place. Repeat with the remaining rectangles.

Mix two tablespoons of boiling water together with the icing sugar until smooth.

Brush all four loaves with milk and coat the crosses with the icing sugar glaze. Sprinkle the coloured sugar strands all over and bake in the oven for 20 minutes until nice and golden.

Leave to cool on a wire rack for at least 1 hour before serving.

Pane di Pasqua con pecorino, miele e salame

EASTER BREAD WITH PECORINO CHEESE, HONEY & SALAMI

Breaking bread together is an ancient gesture, an act of sharing the essential joys of life. This superb puffy bread is a wonderful accompaniment for cold meats and the savoury treats typical of regional Italian food, greedily consumed during the holidays as if there's no tomorrow. It's also great with soup. The proving time is quite long, giving you time to dedicate yourself to your favourite hobbies. Perfect for a rainy Sunday.

Preparation time: 15 minutes plus proving

Cooking time: 30 minutes

Makes 4 loaves

2 tablespoons fast-action dried yeast

1 teaspoon caster sugar

120ml (4fl oz) lukewarm water

1kg (2lb 4oz) strong white flour

50ml (2fl oz) extra virgin olive oil

200g (7oz) pecorino romano cheese, 100g (3½oz) grated and 100g (3½oz) cut into 1-cm (½-inch) cubes

40g (1½oz) sesame seeds

pinch of salt

150g (5½oz) whole Italian salami Milano, cut into 1-cm (½-inch) cubes

100g (3½oz) clear honey

4 garlic cloves, peeled and left whole

Dissolve the yeast and sugar together in the lukewarm water.

Sift the flour into a large bowl. Make a well in the centre, add the yeast mixture and the oil and mix everything together to form a dough. Knead for 5 minutes, then add the grated pecorino, sesame seeds and salt and continue to knead until the dough is smooth and elastic. Add the pecorino and salami pieces, ensuring they are distributed evenly throughout the dough, cover the bowl with a damp tea towel and leave the dough to prove in a warm place for 1½ hours.

Uncover the proven dough and, using a sharp knife, make two cuts about 1cm (½ inch) deep into it in the shape of a cross (this will help delay the proving and develop the flavours within the loaf). Leave to prove for another 1½ hours, then cut again in the same way and leave to prove for a final 1 hour until the dough is twice its original size.

Once the proving is done, add the honey to the bowl and knead it into the bread until it's fully absorbed. Divide the dough into four equal-sized pieces and shape into circular loaves, cutting a cross on top of each. Leave the loaves to rise again for a final 15 minutes.

Preheat the oven to 180°C (350°F), Gas Mark 4. Line an oven tray with baking paper.

Lightly brush the surface of the loaves with water and place a garlic clove on top of each. Transfer to the prepared baking tray and bake in the oven for 30 minutes, or until thoroughly golden.

Remove the loaves from the oven and leave to cool on a wire rack for at least 30 minutes before breaking bread.

Lumaca di pangiallo Romanesco dell'imperatore con gelatina di mandarini

IMPERIAL-STYLE SWEET GOLDEN BREAD WITH CLEMENTINE JELLY

This dessert is associated with the winter solstice on the 21st of December. In the days of the Roman Empire, it was prepared to increase the chances of the sun making a comeback. With my own usual zigzagging between Rome, Paris and London, I bring you my updated version of this old-fashioned treat. Widening the horizon, and bringing it back in style. Roar!

Preparation time: 30 minutes plus chilling, soaking and rising

Cooking time: 30–40 minutes

Serves 8–10

4 tablespoons fast-action dried yeast

190ml (7fl oz) lukewarm milk

800g (1lb 12oz) strong white flour

4 large eggs

150g (5½oz) caster sugar, plus extra to decorate

120g (4oz) unsalted butter, melted

zest of 1 lemon

Filling:

100g (3½oz) raisins

50g (1¾oz) soft dried figs

50g (1¾oz) soft dried prunes, pitted

50g (1¾oz) blanched almonds, roughly chopped

50g (1¾oz) hazelnuts, roughly chopped

80g (3oz) unsalted pistachios, roughly chopped

80g (3oz) chopped walnuts

50g (1¾oz) good-quality dark chocolate (about 75% cocoa solids), very finely chopped

50g (1¾oz) pine nuts

zest of 1 orange

For the clementine jelly, soak the gelatine leaves in a bowl filled with cold water for 10 minutes, then remove and squeeze out the excess water.

Bring the clementine juice, wine and sugar to a simmer in a small saucepan over a low heat. Remove from the heat and mix together with the gelatine leaves until melted. Pour the liquid into 8 small glasses and put them in the refrigerator to cool and set for at least 4 hours.

To make the *pangiallo*, mix the yeast together with the milk in a cup until dissolved, then pour into a large bowl and mix together with 170g (6oz) of the flour to form a smooth, elastic dough. Leave to prove in a warm place for 1 hour until the dough has doubled in size.

Once the dough has proved, beat the eggs and sugar together in a separate bowl until pale and fluffy. Tip the egg mixture into the bowl of a stand mixer with the dough hook attachment added along with the melted butter, remaining flour, lemon zest and proved dough and knead together to form a smooth, sticky dough. Transfer the dough to a bowl, cover with a clean tea towel and leave to rise further in a warm place for 1 hour.

Preheat the oven to 190°C (375°F), Gas Mark 5.

While the dough is rising, prepare the filling. Soak the raisins, figs and prunes in water for 10 minutes, then drain them well. Roughly chop the figs and prunes and place them in a bowl with the raisins, chopped nuts, chocolate, pine nuts, orange zest and raisins, stirring everything together well.

Melt the butter in a small saucepan, add the breadcrumbs and cook, stirring, for a few minutes until lightly toasted. Tip the breadcrumbs into the fruit and nut mixture.

In a separate bowl, beat the egg whites together with a pinch of salt until stiff peaks form. Fold the egg whites along with the beaten yolks into the fruit mixture.

For the egg wash, beat the egg yolk together with the saffron threads in a small bowl.

50g (1³⁄₄oz) unsalted butter

1 tablespoon breadcrumbs (*see* page 262)

3 large eggs, separated and yolks beaten

pinch of salt

Egg wash:

1 egg yolk

10–15 saffron threads

Decoration:

1 x 270-g (9³⁄₄-oz) filo pastry sheet, thawed if frozen

50g (1³⁄₄oz) icing sugar

1 tablespoon water

Clementine jelly:

15g (¹⁄₂oz) fine gelatine leaves

juice of 20 seedless clementines, approx. 250ml (9fl oz)

300ml (¹⁄₂ pint) pink moscato, champagne or other sparkling wine

2 tablespoons caster sugar

30g (1oz) pomegranate seeds

Roll the risen dough out on a lightly floured surface into a 38-cm (15-inch) x 26-cm (10¹⁄₂-inch) rectangle. Spread the filling over the surface of the dough, leaving a 2-cm (³⁄₄-inch) border around the edges, then, starting from one of the longer sides, roll up the dough to form a long sausage. Starting with one end, roll up the sausage into a spiral shape, then gently transfer it to a baking tray. Brush the surface with the egg wash and sprinkle over a little extra sugar.

Bake in the oven for 30–40 minutes until golden brown, then leave to cool on a wire rack.

While the *pangiallo* is cooling, make the decoration. Unroll the filo pastry sheet and cut out about 50–60 star shapes in three different sizes, either using cookie cutters or freestyle, using a small sharp knife. Arrange the pastry stars on an oven dish covered with baking paper – you can brush them with melted butter if you like a crispy effect – and bake for 3–5 minutes until golden, then leave to cool on a wire rack.

In a small pan, gently heat the water together with the icing sugar until dissolved, then mix it with the icing sugar until creamy.

Overlay three stars of different sizes and glue them together with a drop of the icing sugar glaze, then use a little more glaze to fix them to the *pangiallo*. Repeat with the remaining stars until the entire snail is covered.

When ready to serve, remove the jellies from the refrigerator and scatter over the pomegranate seeds. Serve alongside the *pangiallo*, cut into thick slices.

Pesche sciroppate con panna

POACHED PEACHES IN SYRUP WITH CREAM

Ferragosto is a public holiday in Italy, celebrated on the 15th of August, which is also the Feast of the Assumption. All the major cities are deserted as people take a celebratory *gita fuori porta* – literally an excursion outside the city walls. Forget about packing a small picnic to eat under the shade of a tree; no, for an Italian family this means full-on cutlery, cake and trays of lasagne. At the end of the meal you'll be spoon-fed – and I don't mean this figuratively – poached fruit in honeyed syrup. You've just earned yourself a digestif and a nap under the tree. The peaches here need to be stored for a minimum of 15 days before using in order to develop their beautiful flavours, and will keep for up to six months. You could also enjoy these peaches with prosciutto, instead of the usual melon.

Preparation time: 15 minutes plus storing

Cooking time: 35 minutes

Makes 4 x 250-ml (9fl-oz) jars

1kg (2lb 4oz) yellow or white peaches

4 tablespoons lemon juice

1 litre (1¾pints) water

350g (12oz) caster sugar

12 cloves

4 cinnamon sticks

4 star anise

4 vanilla pods

To serve (enough for 4):

300ml (½ pint) whipping cream

small handful of mint leaves (optional)

100g (3½oz) blackberries (optional)

Peel, pit and quarter the peaches, placing the peach pieces in a large bowl of water together with the lemon juice as you go to prevent them from darkening.

Fill a large casserole dish with water and bring it to a boil. Carefully lower the peach quarters into the boiling water and blanch for 2 minutes, then drain and run under cold water to cool.

Once cool, fill the jars with the peach quarters, leaving at a gap of at least 1cm (½ inch) between the top of the peaches and the top of each jar.

Pour the measured water and sugar into a heavy-based saucepan. Bring to a boil, then lower the heat and simmer for 2–3 minutes to form a thick, transparent syrup. Remove from the heat.

Pour the syrup over the peaches to cover completely. Divide the cloves, cinnamon, star anise and vanilla pods between the jars and screw on the jar tops tightly. Invert the jars and leave to cool to room temperature.

Once the jars have cooled, place them in the centre of a large saucepan. Tie the jars together with a clean tea towel (this will prevent them moving around and chipping), cover them with water and bring to a boil. Boil for 30 minutes, then turn off the heat and leave the jars to cool in the pan for a further 30 minutes before removing from the water and drying. Store the jars in a cool, dry place away from sunlight for a minimum of 15 days before using to allow the flavours to fully develop.

When you are ready to enjoy a jar of the peaches, whip the cream until stiff.

Transfer the peaches and a little of their syrup juice into a serving bowl, spoon over the whipped cream and scatter over some mint leaves and blackberries to finish, if you like.

Cotechino in crosta con insalata di finocchi, olive, arance e melograno

CRUSTED COTECHINO WITH FENNEL, OLIVE, ORANGE & POMEGRANATE SALAD

Here I'm paying homage to the British beef Wellington with my Anglo-Italian version of a classic New Year's Eve combination: lentils and *cotechino*, both symbols of abundant good wishes for the year ahead. You can find *cotechino* sausage in most Italian delis, but if you don't want to make the trip, there are also many online suppliers that sell it (I like Melbury & Appleton). Slices of *cotechino* prepared in this way are also delicious dipped in Red Onion Preserve (*see* page 263).

Preparation time: 25 minutes plus cooling

Cooking time: 1½ hours

Serves 6

1 x 500-g (1lb 2-oz) pre-cooked *cotechino* sausage

1 small carrot, finely chopped

1 shallot, finely chopped

1 celery stick, trimmed and finely chopped

small handful of dill fronds, finely chopped

1 rosemary sprig, leaves picked and finely chopped

4 tablespoons extra virgin oil

150g (5½oz) dried brown lentils

20g (¾oz) dried porcini mushrooms (ceps), soaked in 300ml (½ pint) boiling water for at least 10 minutes

1 x 320-g (11½-oz) shortcrust pastry sheet, thawed if frozen

1 teaspoon whipping cream, single cream or milk

1 large egg yolk

salt and pepper

Prepare the *cotechino* following the package instructions or by cooking it in its aluminium wrapping in a large casserole dish of boiling water for 20–30 minutes. Remove the *cotechino* from the water with a slotted spoon and leave it to cool for at least 10 minutes, then extract it from its wrapping. Discard the jelly skin coating the meat and set the *cotechino* aside on a dish.

Preheat the oven to 180°C (350°F), Gas Mark 4. Line an oven tray with baking paper.

Meanwhile, prepare a *soffritto* by sweating the chopped carrot, shallot, celery and herbs together with the oil in a pan over a low heat for 10 minutes. Add the lentils along with the porcini mushrooms and their soaking liquid, bring to a simmer and cook gently for 30–40 minutes until the lentils are soft but retain a little bite. Season with salt and pepper, then tip the mixture into a food processor and blend to a coarse paste. Set aside.

Carefully roll out the pastry sheet and lay it in the centre of the lined oven tray. Place the *cotechino* in the middle of the pastry sheet, spoon over the lentil paste to cover it evenly and roll the pastry around the sausage to form a tight log. Seal the edges of the pastry, cutting off any excess (you can use this to make decorative shapes to cover the pastry crust – I love to make leaves).

Mix the cream and egg yolk together to make a wash and use it brush all over the surface of the pastry. Bake the *cotechino* in the oven for 30 minutes until the pastry crust is golden.

While the *cotechino* is cooking, prepare the salad. Soak the raisins in a small bowl filled with water for 10 minutes. Drain and set aside.

Squeeze one of the oranges and strain the juice. With a sharp knife, remove and discard the peel from the remaining orange and cut the orange flesh into 1-cm (½-inch) slices.

Salad:

30g (1oz) raisins

2 oranges

160g (6oz) baby chicory

1 fennel bulb

100g (3½oz) black olives, pitted

110g (4oz) pomegranate seeds

30g (1oz) pine nuts

30g (1oz) walnut pieces

3 tablespoons extra virgin olive oil

pinch of salt

Trim and thinly slice the baby chicory and the fennel bulb, setting aside the leafy fennel fronds, and arrange the slices in a salad bowl together with the orange slices, olives, pomegranate seeds, pine nuts, walnut pieces and raisins.

Finely chop the fennel fronds and combine with the oil, orange juice and salt to make a dressing. Toss the salad in the dressing to coat before serving with the pastry-wrapped *cotechino*, cut into 1.5-cm (⅝ -inch) slices.

Pesce finto di Natale

CHRISTMAS 'FISH'

Not far from the Pantheon stands Sant'Ignazio Church, built in the grand Baroque style. When I walk past its massive Corinthian pilasters I think I'm seeing double; I am mesmerized by the richly adorned altar and stare up at the cupola – it looks as if a bright blue sky is awaiting me outside. I can't believe my eyes, but then again I shouldn't. The cupola is a *trompe l'œil* painting. It's a trick of the eye. So too is this festive dish – a fake Christmas 'fish' that is fun to make with kids. If you have a suitable fish mould, so much the better, alternatively, you can shape it according to your own taste. Make it spectacularly Roman or make it all yours.

Preparation time: 10 minutes plus chilling

Cooking time: 20 minutes

Serves 8

1kg (2lb 4oz) Desiree, Mozart or other waxy salad potatoes, peeled and cut into 1-cm (½-inch) cubes

500g (1lb 2oz) tinned tuna in spring water

8 anchovy fillets in olive oil, drained

100g (3½oz) pitted green olives, plus 1 extra to garnish

2 teaspoons dried oregano

50g (1¾oz) unsalted butter, softened

1 teaspoon capers in vinegar, drained

zest of 1 lemon

1 medium cucumber, cut into 5-mm (¼-inch) circles

1 medium carrot, cut into 5-mm (¼-inch) circles

250g (9oz) mayonnaise

salt

Bring a saucepan of salted water to a boil. Add the potatoes, cover and simmer over a medium-high heat for 20 minutes, or until the potatoes are entirely soft.

Meanwhile, put the tuna, anchovies, olives, oregano, butter and capers in a food processor and blend together to a thick, creamy paste. Stir in the lemon zest and set aside.

Drain the potato pieces, tip them into a large bowl and coarsely mash them with a fork. Add the tuna paste and mix everything together well.

Spoon the tuna and potato mixture into a fish mould and turn it out onto the centre of a large serving plate. Alternatively, spoon the mixture into the centre of the plate and sculpt it into a fish shape using your hands.

Arrange the cucumber and carrot slices over the 'fish' like scales and add an olive as an eye, then use a spatula to coat the surface evenly with the mayonnaise.

Transfer to the refrigerator and leave to chill for at least 1 hour before serving.

Castagnole di carnevale alla Romana

ROMAN-STYLE CARNIVAL SWEET DOUGH BALLS

In the musical *Rugantino*, the title character asks the city of Rome itself to be his partner in crime as he tries to seduce a married woman. '*Sceji tutte le stelle più brillarelle che c'hai, e un friccico de luna tutta pè noi.*' 'Light up all your bright stars, and a glimmer of moonlight just for us.' But then again, everyone allows themselves transgressions during Carnival, a time when people from all walks of life would traditionally cross each other's paths, a *castagnola* in their hand as a matchmaker. Nine months later, the nuns would find a basket with a newborn on their doorstep. Here, I chart my love for uncompromised gluttonous pleasures.

Preparation time: 10 minutes

Cooking time: 15 minutes

Makes 30 *castagnole*

2 eggs

140g (5oz) plain flour

60g (2¹/₄oz) cornflour

1 vanilla pod, split lengthways and seeds scraped

zest of 1 lemon

1 teaspoon baking powder

2 tablespoons extra virgin olive oil

50g (1³/₄oz) icing sugar, plus extra for dusting

1 tablespoon Roman-Style Sambuca (*see* page 271), Marsala or sherry

pinch of salt

Preheat the oven to 180°C (350°F), Gas Mark 4. Line a baking tray with baking paper.

Beat the eggs together in a large bowl until fluffy. Sift over the flour, add the cornflour, vanilla seeds, lemon zest, baking powder, oil, icing sugar and liqueur and mix everything together thoroughly to form a smooth, sticky dough. Add the salt, cover with a clean tea towel and leave the dough to rest for 5 minutes.

Once rested, roll the dough out on a lightly floured surface into a long sausage shape. Slice the dough sausage into 2-cm (1-inch) pieces and shape each into a hazelnut-sized ball.

Arrange the dough balls on the prepared baking tray, leaving about 1cm (¹/₂ inch) space between each, and bake for 15 minutes until the *castagnole* have risen by about a third and are lightly golden. Transfer to a wire rack and leave to cool for 10 minutes.

Once cool, arrange the *castagnole* on a serving dish in a pyramid shape before dusting them with a coating of icing sugar to finish.

Chapter 9
CAKES & CO.

Separated from Rome's historical centre by a bridge, Trastevere is a different world: artists, artisans and intellectuals populate a district where religious processions alternate with gay pride marches and food festivals. The fountain of Piazza Trilussa was moved here from the other side of the river in an act of cultural munificence – a present to a part of town that, in comparison with the rest, had little in the way of monuments.

The Grand Tour exposed the offspring of wealthy families to the cultural legacy of Rome. More often than not, at night these young men would venture into the city's less savoury districts, of which Trastevere was one, to play cards and gamble. If a cheat was discovered, the police were called and the guilty party would spend the night in a cell – or *al fresco*, as the Romans say.

For a long time, my favourite spot in Trastevere was a *pasticceria* that had been there for almost 100 years. Virginia, the lady who welcomed me to this little *confetteria*, embodied the essence of the Roman *matrona*: a rather imposing woman, in charge of the family. She always made sure I ate enough, and offered me her beloved son's latest gastronomic creations. When she first told me about him, I imagined a young boy working wonders at the back of the shop. When she finally introduced me to this supposed child prodigy of baking, I found myself, much to my surprise, staring up at a guy of about six foot five.

The walls of the shop were covered with this man's surreal paintings, each resolving one of the many Roman historical dilemmas, the same ones one could often observe being fiercely debated just outside the *pasticceria*. I was always open to the eccentric points of view provided by Virginia on various topics, a fork in her hand to emphatically make her point and a piece of Grandma's Custard Pie (*see* page 238) on her hand-painted china plate, from the protests of 1968 to the separation of church and state. Sadly, this historic place closed in May 2015, due to the sudden deaths of both *signora* Virginia and her son. They left in gentle silence and with the scent of chocolate slowly fading away. I am left with memories of a miniature of Rome painted by the scrupulous hand of a talented mummy's boy, who made the best Castagnaccio (*see* page 245) in town. *Laudemus tortam.*

Fruttini gelato

ICE CREAM FRUITS

Here is a scrumptious dessert you can indulge in without having to loosen your belt. I love to get these perfumed morsels – nothing more than fruity ice cream served in the fruit's own frozen skin – out of the freezer at the end of an impromptu dinner. All you need to do is remove the flesh of the fruit and then freeze its shell, which will serve as the vessel for the fruity ice cream itself. Serve them in a bowl as if they were simply fruit – your friends will be amazed to find the ice cream surprise inside!

Preparation time: 40 minutes plus freezing

Serves 8

4 figs

4 small pears

12 large cherries or
    12 blackberries plus a handful of
    blackberries for the filling
500ml (18fl oz) vanilla ice cream

3 tablespoons whipping cream

small handful of mint leaves

Start off by preparing the fruits. Cut the figs and pears into halves and very gently excavate the flesh with the help of a teaspoon, setting the flesh aside in separate bowls. Repeat the same process with the cherries, if using, placing the flesh in a separate bowl and taking off the stalks and removing the stones as you go. Cut 12 blackberries, if using, into halves and set aside. Place the remaining handful of blackberries in a separate bowl and blitz them together.

Place the fruit 'shells' in a dish, transfer to the freezer and leave for 2 hours until frozen solid.

Add a third of the ice cream along with a tablespoon of whipping cream, if using, to each of the fruit bowls. Mix together well to give you three different fruity ice creams.

Remove the fruit 'shells' from the freezer one type of fruit at a time. Fill the halves of each fruit with their respective ice cream, then sandwich them together to make them whole again. Return to the freezer for at least 30 minutes, or until needed.

To serve, arrange the frozen fruits in a fruit bowl and decorate with the mint leaves.

Meringona alla Romana con salsa di arance

ROMAN-STYLE MERINGUE WITH ORANGE SAUCE

There's the candyfloss sold on Piazza Navona as Christmas approaches, and then there's the much more civilized Roman meringue. Romans make enormous meringues, reaching almost impossible heights. Why? Because once the Romans actually get around to doing, they often overdo. The secret to making a successful meringue: make sure to add your sugar a little at a time and keep whisking. Cloud-shaped Roman megalomania.

Preparation time: 15 minutes

Cooking time: 1 hour 15 minutes plus cooling

Serves 6

150g (5½oz) icing sugar

150g (5½oz) caster sugar

6 extra-large egg whites

pinch of salt

1 tablespoon cornflour

Orange sauce:

juice of 4 oranges

4 tablespoons icing sugar

2 tablespoons orange blossom
    water

To serve:

300ml (½ pint) whipping cream

2 tablespoons chopped mint leaves

2 tablespoons rose petals or edible
    red glitter

Preheat the oven to 150°C (300°F), Gas Mark 2. Line a baking tray with baking paper.

Combine the two sugars in a small bowl.

Put the egg whites in a large bowl with a pinch of salt. Whisk the egg whites together, adding the cornflour after a few minutes, until they form stiff peaks. Keep whisking vigorously and start adding the sugar mix a tablespoon at a time (it's imperative to add the sugar gradually – no-one wants a watery meringue) until the mixture is glossy and thick.

With the help of a spatula or 2 large spoons, form six billowy meringues on the prepared baking tray, gently flicking the spatula or spoon as you deposit the mixture on the tray to give the meringues a pointed, spiky finish.

Bake the meringues for 1 hour until pale and creamy in colour, then switch off the oven, open the door slightly and leave to cool in the oven for 15 minutes.

While the meringues are cooling, make the orange sauce. Pour the orange juice into a small saucepan, add the icing sugar and orange blossom water and bring to a boil. Lower the heat and simmer for 5 minutes, until the sauce is syrupy and smooth.

To serve, whip the cream until stiff and stir in the chopped mint. Divide the cream between individual serving plates, spooning it into the centre of each plate. Place the meringues on top of the cream and spoon over the sauce, finishing each plate with a scattering of rose petals or edible glitter.

Torta al cioccolato, amaretti e tutti frutti

CHOCOLATE, AMARETTI & TUTTI FRUTTI CAKE

One day, as I was eating my chocolate cake in a tiny family-run restaurant in Rome, I saw a large group of people happily eating, drinking and being merry. Then they started leaving one by one, trying to go unnoticed. Eventually, only the man at the head of the table remained. The waiter went up to him, only to hear this fateful sentence: 'May I come by tomorrow to settle *la dolorosa*?' ('The painful one' – an Italian synonym for the bill.) 'No, *dotto*' (all Roman restaurateurs address their clientele as 'doctor'), 'either you pay now or I will kick your ass.' Sometimes, eating at home is so much safer. Roman faces, *tutti frutti*.

Preparation time: 20 minutes

Cooking time: 1 hour

Serves 8

200g (7oz) good-quality dark chocolate (about 70% cocoa solids), roughly chopped

170g (6oz) unsalted butter

pinch of salt

350ml (12fl oz) rum

4 Conference pears, peeled, cored and cut into wedges

1 large banana, sliced

100g (3½oz) light brown sugar

4 large eggs, separated

1 tablespoon baking powder

100ml (3½fl oz) lukewarm milk

100g (3½oz) amaretti biscuits, broken into crumbs

1 tablespoon chopped thyme leaves, fresh or dried

200g (7oz) plain flour, sifted

150g (5½oz) stoneless black cherries in syrup

Preheat the oven to 200°C (400°F), Gas Mark 6. Line the bottom and sides of a 22-cm (8½-inch) springform cake tin with baking paper.

Melt the chocolate pieces together with half the butter and a pinch of salt in a bowl set over a saucepan of lightly simmering water or in a microwave. Leave to cool.

Place a large non-stick frying pan over a high heat, add the rum and pear wedges and cook for 10–15 minutes, adding the banana slices halfway through cooking and turning occasionally, until the liquid has evaporated and the fruit is golden and caramelized. Set aside.

In a large bowl, beat half the sugar together with the egg yolks until pale, creamy and doubled in volume. Dissolve the baking powder in the milk and add to the bowl along with the melted chocolate, remaining butter, amaretti crumbs, thyme and flour, stirring everything together to form a batter.

In a separate bowl, whisk together the egg whites with a pinch of salt for 5 minutes until they form stiff peaks. Whisking all the while, gradually add the remaining sugar, a tablespoon at a time, until the mixture is glossy and thick. Gently fold the egg white mix into the batter with a spatula.

Pour half the batter into the prepared mould. Spread over the caramelized fruit mix evenly, then cover with the remaining batter.

Bake in the oven for 10 minutes, then lower the heat to 170°C (340°F), Gas Mark 3 and bake for a further 50 minutes until the surface is cracked and a toothpick or cake tester inserted into the centre of the cake comes out clean. Remove the cake from the oven and leave to cool on a wire rack for 30 minutes before turning out onto a serving plate. Spoon the syrupy black cherries over the cake's surface before serving.

Semifreddo ai cantucci e Vin Santo

ALMOND BISCUIT & SWEET WINE SEMIFREDDO

This dense, crumbly dessert is halfway between sorbet and gelato, but without the fuss of using a special ice cream machine, ice cubes and all that jazz. A pudding as fluffy as the Roman clouds when they gather spectacularly, accompanied by swooping flocks of starlings. You can catch sight of this aerial display around mid-October, as the leaves start to fall and fill the tree-lined streets of this endearing city. As an alternative to the crunchy almond *cantucci*, I also like to use plain digestive biscuits, combined with a handful of hazelnuts I've toasted for a few minutes in a small pan.

Preparation time: 30 minutes plus freezing

Serves 8

3 large eggs, separated

50g (1³/₄oz) sugar

pinch of fine salt

400ml (14fl oz) whipping cream

1 tablespoon lemon juice

400g (14oz) cantucci biscuits, crushed

120ml (4fl oz) Vin Santo, Marsala or Madeira

170g (6oz) blackberries (optional), fresh or frozen

Line a 900-g (2-lb) loaf tin with clingfilm, allowing it to overhang the sides (this will make it easy to remove the semifreddo from the mould when it's ready).

In a large bowl, beat the egg yolks with the sugar until the mixture is pale, creamy and almost doubled in size. In a second bowl, beat together the egg whites with a pinch of salt until stiff peaks form. In a third bowl, whisk the cream until soft peaks form.

Add the egg whites to the sugar and egg yolks, then add the whipped cream, folding gently from top to bottom. Gently fold the lemon juice and a quarter of the crushed biscuits into the creamy mixture.

Tip the remaining crushed biscuits into a small bowl, pour over the Vin Santo and mix together well.

Fill the prepared mould first with a layer of the soaked biscuit pieces, then a layer of the creamy mixture. Keep alternating these layers, making sure to finish off with a layer of *cantucci*, until all the ingredients are used, then transfer to the freezer and leave for at least 4 hours to freeze until firm.

Take the semifreddo out of the freezer 10–15 minutes before serving to allow it to soften slightly. When ready to serve, flip the mould upside down and turn the semifreddo out onto an oval dish. Scatter a few blackberries over the surface, if you like, and serve cut into thick slices.

Torta della nonna

GRANDMA'S CUSTARD PIE

When I was 13 or 14, I started spending all my non-school hours in the kitchen – my great grandmother's sanctuary, which I had been forbidden to enter until then, as no messy children were allowed. I felt drawn to the mysterious calm this special room infused me with. From my family I inherited a recipe book filled with secrets that I started studying. On rainy days, I loved to chase away the gloom by putting my hands in some sweet dough. What I love about kneading dough is that you're bringing your body heat to work with the gluten and the flour: a real collaboration between you and the food. Just like my granny taught me by example and involvement, drawing me into the kitchen. From then on, I never wanted to be anywhere else. *La torta della nonna* is one of the most heart-warming and easiest cakes in the Roman baking repertoire. I've added my own twist in the form of white chocolate, for extra depth of flavour.

Preparation time: 15 minutes plus resting

Cooking time: 40 minutes

Serves 8

400g (14oz) plain flour

200g (7oz) unsalted butter, chilled and cut into 1-cm (1/2-inch) cubes, plus extra for greasing

pinch of salt

150g (5 1/2oz) caster sugar

4 egg yolks

zest of 1 lemon

50g (1 3/4oz) pine nuts

50g (1 3/4oz) icing sugar

30g (1oz) white chocolate, to decorate

Custard:

4 egg yolks

50g (1 3/4oz) plain flour

500ml (18fl oz) milk

100g (3 1/2oz) caster sugar

zest of 1 lemon

50g (1 3/4oz) white chocolate, broken into chips

For the custard, whisk together the egg yolks, flour, milk, sugar and lemon zest in a saucepan. Heat gently, stirring continuously, for 10 minutes over low heat, or until the custard is thick enough to coat the back of a spoon. Stir the white chocolate into the hot custard to melt and mix together well. Remove from the heat and set aside to cool.

Place the flour in a bowl, add the butter and salt and rub in with the fingertips until the mixture resembles coarse breadcrumbs. Form a well in the centre and pour over the sugar, egg yolks and lemon zest and mix everything together by hand briefly to form a smooth pastry dough (try to avoid working the pastry for too long, as you'll melt the butter, and no one wants a soggy pastry). Wrap the dough in clingfilm, transfer to the refrigerator and leave to rest for 30 minutes.

Preheat the oven to 180°C (350°F), Gas Mark 4. Grease a 23-cm (9-inch) tart tin with butter.

Once rested, divide the dough into two equal-sized pieces. On a floured surface, roll each dough piece into a 25-cm (10-inch) disc using a rolling pin. Line the base and sides of the prepared tin with one of the dough discs, pressing it down gently to fix it in place and trimming off any excess.

Pour the custard into the tin, cover it with the second pastry disc and pinch the edges together using your fingers to seal the pie, trimming off the excess pastry as necessary. Sprinkle over the pine nuts and icing sugar, then bake in the oven for 30 minutes until the pastry is golden and the pine nuts are well toasted.

Remove the pie from the oven and leave to cool on a wire rack for 1 hour. Grate over some white chocolate to decorate before serving.

Crostata ricotta e cioccolato come al ghetto

GHETTO-STYLE RICOTTA & CHOCOLATE PIE

The ruins of the Roman Forum encompass the various eras of Rome – there are temples, the Christian basilica of Santa Francesca Romana, the remnants of triumphal arches and the Colosseum in the background. And then there is *crostata ricotta e cioccolato*, one of Rome's hidden splendours. Just steps from the Teatro Marcello, tucked away on the corner of the road leading to Portico d'Ottavia, the centre of Rome's Jewish Ghetto, there's a *forno* that is famous for its ricotta and chocolate tart. This eternal city is a collection of different cities, one inside the other, and this recipe is a collection of flavours inside a golden, crusty shell.

Preparation time: 15 minutes plus resting

Cooking time: 45 minutes

Serves 6

knob of unsalted butter, for greasing

1 egg yolk, beaten, for brushing

400g (14oz) ricotta

4 tablespoons caster sugar

zest of 1 lemon

30g (1oz) dark chocolate flakes or coarsely grated dark chocolate

Pastry:

2 eggs

120g (4oz) icing sugar

90g (3¼oz) sunflower oil

1 teaspoon baking powder

140g (5oz) spelt flour, sifted

250g (9oz) plain flour, sifted

30g (1oz) black sesame seeds

Grease a 20-cm (8-inch) circular pie tin with butter.

For the pastry, whisk the eggs together with the icing sugar, oil and baking powder in a large mixing bowl or the bowl of a stand mixer with the dough hook attachment added. Add the sifted flours and sesame seeds and mix together briefly to form a delicate, wet dough.

Take a third of the pastry dough and wrap it in aluminium foil. Press small walnut-sized balls of the remaining pastry into the pie tin to cover the bottom and the sides. Transfer both the tin and the foil-wrapped pastry to the refrigerator and leave to rest for 30 minutes.

Preheat the oven to 170°C (340°F), Gas Mark 3.

Once rested, cover the pastry case with baking paper and fill with dried beans. Bake blind for 20 minutes. Remove the pie tin from the oven, tip out the beans and take out the paper. Brush the pastry with the beaten egg yolk and bake for a further 2–3 minutes, until lightly golden. Remove from the oven and leave to cool for 15 minutes.

Increase the oven temperature to 180°C (350°F), Gas Mark 4.

Mix together the ricotta, sugar and lemon zest in a bowl or a food processor until smooth and creamy. Fold in the chocolate flakes, then pour the chocolate and ricotta mixture into the cooled pastry case and level the filling off with the back of a spoon.

Take the reserved chilled pastry out of the refrigerator and crumble it into small pieces with your fingertips. Scatter the pastry crumbs evenly over the surface of the pie and bake in the oven for 20 minutes, until the ricotta filling is firm and slightly cracked and the pastry crumbs are golden. Leave to cool on a wire rack before enjoying at any time of day (or night).

Tiramisù al limone

LEMON TIRAMISÙ

There's nothing like giving a makeover to a classic dish – tradition with a twist. After all, in order to survive, traditions need to suit the modern sensibilities of those who still follow them. Tiramisù literally means 'pick-me-up' and this dessert is all about revelling in the joys of the kitchen. If you have time, make some homemade mascarpone: you'll need a food thermometer and 24 hours' patience. Caution: this could become addictive. Don't say I didn't warn you.

Preparation time: 15 minutes plus chilling

Cooking time: 15 minutes for the mascarpone

Serves 6

6 large egg yolks

6 tablespoons caster sugar

500g (1lb 2oz) mascarpone cheese, store-bought or homemade (see below)

zest and juice of 1 lemon

1 tablespoon limoncello liqueur

300ml (½ pint) full-fat or semi-skimmed milk

250g (9oz) Dunking Biscuits (*see* page 32) or ladyfingers

100g (3½oz) unsalted pistachios

250g (9oz) mixed berries, to decorate

Homemade mascarpone:

1 litre (1¾ pints) whipping cream

2 tablespoons lemon juice

For the homemade mascarpone, pour the cream into a saucepan over a low heat and bring to a temperature of 85°C (185°F), whisking all the while. Once the desired temperature has been reached, gradually add the lemon juice, whisking continuously, and continue to whisk for a further 5 minutes, or until the cream has thickened enough to coat the back of a spoon. Remove from the heat and leave to cool for 15 minutes.

Line a colander with cheesecloth and suspend over a bowl. Pour over the thickened cream and leave to rest at room temperature for 1 hour, then transfer the colander and bowl to the refrigerator and leave to chill for 24 hours. Spoon the mascarpone into an airtight container until ready to use (it will keep for up to 3–4 days in the refrigerator).

To make the tiramisù, whisk the egg yolks together with the sugar in a bowl until pale and creamy. Add the mascarpone and mix together well, then stir in the lemon juice, zest and limoncello.

Pour the milk into a shallow bowl. Briefly dunk the biscuits in the milk for no more than a second per side (you want the biscuits to absorb a little of the liquid but still be firm). Line the base of a large oval dish with a layer of the milk-soaked biscuits and cover with a layer of the mascarpone mixture. Continue to layer in this fashion, finishing with a final layer of cream.

Cover the tiramisù carefully with clingfilm and transfer to the refrigerator for at least 1 hour to chill and set. Blend the pistachios in a food processor or spice grinder to a fine powder and scatter over the tiramisù with the mixed berries before serving.

Torta di castagne e mele con farina alle nocciole
e arance candite

APPLE, CHESTNUT & HAZELNUT CAKE WITH CANDIED ORANGES

Roman fashion never goes out of fashion. World-famous designers have carved their signatures all over the city by staging their fashion shows in breathtaking settings, from the courtyards of private palazzos to the Spanish Steps. Today, those fashion entrepreneurs who cherish their city are donating funds to help preserve historical monuments such as the Colosseum. Times change and so do methods, with a common intent: to radiate splendour. You'll enjoy this cake, which mixes flavours and textures, like a stroll along Via Condotti.

Preparation time: 15 minutes

Cooking time: 1 hour 40 minutes

Serves 8

knob of unsalted butter, for greasing

150g (5½oz) plain flour, plus extra for dusting

peeled zest of 1 large orange, cut into 1-cm (½-inch) strips

2 Bramley or other cooking apples

1 tablespoon lemon juice

120ml (4fl oz) Marsala wine

85g (3oz) light brown sugar

200g (7oz) hazelnuts

3 large eggs

130g (4½oz) caster sugar

6 tablespoons extra virgin olive oil

2 tablespoons baking powder

100ml (3½fl oz) lukewarm milk

100g (3½oz) canned whole chestnuts, roughly chopped

Preheat the oven to 200°C (400°F), Gas Mark 6. Grease a 23-cm (9-inch) cake tin with butter and dust with flour.

Place the orange zest slices in a saucepan and cover with cold water. Put over a high heat and bring to a boil, then drain. Repeat this process twice more, then remove the orange zest from the pan.

Peel and core the two apples. Cut one of the apples lengthways into quarters and then each of the quarters into thin crescent-shaped slices. Place the apple slices in a bowl of water together with the lemon juice to prevent them from browning. Cut the other apple into 1-cm (½-inch) cubes.

Put the apple cubes into a small non-stick frying pan along with the wine and two-thirds of the brown sugar. Gently heat, stirring, for 10 minutes, until the apple pieces have softened but still retain their shape. Remove from the heat and set aside.

Blend the hazelnuts in a food processor to a fine powder.

Whisk the eggs together with the caster sugar in a large bowl for 3 minutes until light and fluffy. Sift over the flour and hazelnut powder and mix together well, gradually adding the olive oil as you go. Dissolve the baking powder in the milk and add to the bowl along with the apples and chestnuts, stirring everything together to form a thick, smooth batter.

Pour the batter into the prepared cake tin, then carefully arrange the apple slices in a circular pattern on the surface. Scatter over the orange zest slices and sprinkle over the remaining brown sugar.

Bake in the oven for 10 minutes, then lower the temperature to 170°C (340°F), Gas Mark 3 and bake for a further 50 minutes, until the apple slices are golden and a skewer or toothpick inserted into the centre of the cake comes out clean. Leave to cool in the tin on a wire rack for at least 30 minutes before serving. Enjoy with a cup of tea.

Castagnaccio

CHESTNUT FLOUR CAKE

One of the main street foods of Rome is *caldarrosta*, roast chestnuts, which never go out of fashion. You see the vendors keeping warm by their grills on street corners, with a cup of sweet wine in one hand and a piping hot roast chestnut in the other. While this is not a recipe for roast chestnuts, it does feature the same shiny brown nut as its protagonist. Best of all, it has a curiously romantic story. Traditionally, rosemary leaves were added to the cake as a love potion: the boy who ate a slice offered to him by a girl would immediately fall in love with her and consequently marry her.

This cake is made with chestnut flour, which can be found in speciality stores (I like to buy mine online from Shipton Mill) and will keep in a suitable container for up to 3 days.

Preparation time: 10 minutes

Cooking time: 1 hour

Serves 6

6 tablespoons extra virgin olive oil, plus extra for greasing

3 eggs

150g (5½oz) caster sugar

200g (7oz) chestnut flour

200g (7oz) plain flour

2 teaspoons baking powder

400ml (14fl oz) lukewarm milk

30g (1oz) dark cocoa powder

1 vanilla pod, split lengthways and seeds scraped

3 rosemary sprigs, leaves picked

50g (2¼oz) pine nuts

50g (1¾oz) raisins, soaked in warm water for 10 minutes and drained

20g (¾oz) fennel seeds

20g (¾oz) pumpkin seeds

30g (1oz) icing sugar

Preheat the oven to 180°C (350°F), Gas Mark 4. Grease a 20-cm (8-inch) cake tin with a little olive oil.

Beat the eggs and sugar together in a bowl with an electric whisk for 5 minutes or until light and fluffy.

Sift over the flours and baking powder and stir them into the egg mixture along with the milk, cocoa powder, olive oil and vanilla seeds to form a batter. Add the rosemary leaves and pine nuts, reserving a small handful of each, along with the raisins, fennel seeds and pumpkin seeds and mix everything together well.

Pour the batter into the prepared cake tin. Scatter the remaining rosemary leaves and pine nuts over the surface of the cake and bake for 1 hour, or until the cake is cracked on the surface, a skewer or toothpick inserted into the centre comes out clean and the pine nuts are golden brown.

Dust with icing sugar and serve warm or cold.

Rotolo ricotta e visciole

SOUR CHERRY & RICOTTA ROLL CAKE

Some varieties of sweet cherry need help with pollination, and every spring, that is the role that sour cherries play in nature. *Ricotta di pecora* (sheep's milk ricotta) has long been a great resource of the countryside around Rome, a region that used to contain more sheep than people. In 1817 Pope Pius VII used a document called a *motu proprio*, which means 'on his own impulse', to extend the boundaries of the municipality of Rome, giving these under-populated territories new recognition.
I created this recipe on the occasion of a blog exchange with Elizabeth Minett, of *Haut Appétit*. In the same way, if you can forgive the blasphemy, I give new recognition to this ancient combination of ingredients – a feast for the eye and the stomach, as if by papal decree.

Preparation time: 15 minutes

Cooking time: 15 minutes

Serves 6

4 eggs, plus 1 yolk

120g (4oz) caster sugar

2 tablespoons cocoa powder

120ml (4fl oz) vegetable oil

135g (5oz) plain flour

1 teaspoon baking powder

150g (5½oz) sour cherry jam

250g (9oz) ricotta cheese

50g (1¾oz) icing sugar

100g (3½oz) mixed berries (redcurrants, blackberries, rasperries, strawberries)

Preheat the oven to 180°C (350°F), Gas Mark 4. Line a 35 x 22-cm (14 x 8½-inch) baking tin or a baking tray with a sheet of greaseproof paper.

Whisk the eggs and extra yolk in a bowl together with the caster sugar for 5 minutes until everything is light and fluffy. Gradually whisk in the cocoa powder and vegetable oil before sifting over the flour and baking powder, whisking all the while, to form a smooth batter.

Pour the batter into the prepared tin to form a thin layer, levelling it off with the back of a spoon. Bake for 15 minutes, or until the sponge is lightly golden and springs back when lightly pressed with your fingertips, then remove the sponge from the oven and leave to cool in the tin for a couple of minutes only (you want to be able to roll the cake while still hot so it doesn't break).

Once cooled slightly, remove the sponge from the tin and spread the cherry jam evenly over its surface, then cover with the ricotta. With one of the shortest edges facing you, roll the sponge up tightly into a log, using the paper as a guide.

Sprinkle the roll with icing sugar and decorate with clusters of berries to serve.

Chapter 10 PROVISIONS

Every September you'll hear inviting sizzling noises escaping the kitchen windows of Rome. This time of year is all about stocking up the pantry for winter, and people will regularly share their handmade goodies. To me, this is yet further proof of how much cooking is an integral part of people's lives here – not just a hobby, but a highly valued form of communication. A handmade gift is the most genuine gesture.

When I enter Teresa's kitchen on Via del Pellegrino, she greets me with a kiss while handing me a bottle of *sugo* (*see* page 254). 'You simply must have this sauce. Here!' she says, with ample gesticulation. Her kitchen with its green Formica tables is about to be filled with joy as she offers me some cheese accompanied by Red Onion Preserve (*see* page 263) and a few Breadsticks (*see* page 258). 'At least you'll eat something, you're a bag of bones, sweetheart', she says, convinced that I'm somehow malnourished. Teresa, like many Roman women of her generation, loathes the young people's habit of consuming only three courses per meal. In her day, there would be an assortment of antipasti followed by *primi piatti* (pasta and rice), *secondi piatti* (meat and fish), *terzi piatti* (salad and cheese), *quarti piatti* (fruit) and *quinti piatti* (dessert). Twice a day, every day. And it is considered bad manners to leave even one piece of pasta on your plate. Never, ever.

There are still a few trattorias in Rome that perfectly correspond to my idea of off-the-beaten-track Roman food. Take for example Mami Trilussa, a temple of gluttony where you'll be served your carbonara directly in the pan, to make dunking the bread easier. For the best meat in town, I head to Cesare al Casaletto, a hidden gem just off the town's historical centre. And when it comes to flawless tiramisù, I know that Settimio all'Arancio will never disappoint. Then, I'll stroll around the Roman triangle (Via Condotti, Via del Corso, Piazza di Spagna) and I know how I stand: still and in total veneration.

Restaurants in Rome – the trick lies in knowing where to find them. Go for a walk, don't let yourself be lured into a restaurant by a guy standing outside it calling out to you, and don't be afraid to enter the more modest ones: it's often in the less showy venues that you'll find tradition on display.

Carciofini sott'olio

ARTICHOKES IN OIL

I love the versatility of artichokes. Plenty of otherwise boring dishes acquire that much-needed extra depth of flavour thanks to their addition. There are hundreds of time-consuming ways to prepare these irresistible artichoke hearts, but why should it take a lifetime to make them when it only takes a couple of minutes to eat them? This recipe is a quick and easy compromise – another way of having your artichoke and eating it, too.

Preparation time: 5 minutes plus marinating

Makes 2 x 250-ml (9fl-oz) jars

4 tablespoons lemon juice

120ml (4fl oz) extra virgin olive oil

1 teaspoon white wine vinegar

1 tablespoon salt

15 black peppercorns

1 teaspoon dried oregano

handful of mint leaves, chopped

250g (9oz) canned artichoke hearts in water, drained

Put the lemon juice, olive oil, vinegar, salt, peppercorns, oregano and mint into a large food bag. Seal the bag and shake for 1 minute to mix everything together well.

Open the bag and add the artichoke hearts, then seal again and shake for a further 1–2 minutes, until the artichokes are evenly coated in oil.

Spoon the artichoke hearts into sterilized jars (*see* page 254) and pour over the oil and vinegar mixture. Leave the artichokes to marinate for at least 2 hours before serving or store in a cool, dark place for up to 5 days.

Sugo passepartout per conserve, pizza e pasta

PASSEPARTOUT TOMATO SAUCE FOR PRESERVES, PIZZA & PASTA

Making your own tomato sauce is delightfully easy – the uncompromising honesty of the flavours will make you wonder why you waited so long to try it. I suggest you go for organic tomatoes ripened on the vine, if possible, though any vine tomato is fine.

Heat some oil in a pan, sweat some garlic and onion and then add this juicy sauce. Let it reduce for about 20 minutes, stirring in a little boiling water halfway through, and that's it. The next time that need for a succulent tomato sauce arises, you'll open the jar, letting out all those Mediterranean flavours. Get ready to enter a new stage of kitchen intoxication.

Preparation time: 5 minutes

Cooking time: 6 minutes

Makes 2 x 750-ml (1¼-pint) jars:

12 medium-sized firm vine
  tomatoes

2 tablespoons chopped basil,
  thyme or rosemary leaves

salt

Start by sterilizing the jars. Preheat the oven to 120°C (250°F), Gas Mark ½. Wash the jars and their lids in hot, soapy water, rinse thoroughly and place in the oven for 10 minutes to dry completely.

Bring a large saucepan of salted water to a boil. Lower in the tomatoes and cook for 6 minutes or until the tomato skins just start to come away from the flesh. Remove the tomatoes with a slotted spoon, transfer to a food processor and blend together with your chosen herb for 20 seconds or so to form a smooth sauce.

Spoon the sauce into the sterilized jars and screw the lids on firmly to close. Tie the jars together with a clean tea towel (this will prevent them moving around and chipping), put them into the saucepan upside down and return the water to a boil. Boil for 30 minutes, then turn off the heat and leave the jars to cool in the pan for a further 30 minutes before removing from the water and drying.

Store the jars in a cool, dry place away from sunlight and keep for up to 6 months.

Tozzetti della Tuscia con semi di chia

TUSCAN TOZZETTI BISCUITS WITH CHIA SEEDS

Sprawling is the archetypal after-lunch activity in Rome. After all, modern office life can prove hard, with the usual working day lasting between 4 and 6 hours, broken up by numerous modified coffee siestas, consisting of a shot of espresso with grappa, accompanied by a biscuit and the latest gossip. I love to make these twice-baked crunchy biscuits for special occasions. Dip them in any sweet wine you fancy – they'll make for a wonderful midday snack, waking you up from within. Better than delicious, they're Romanicious.

Preparation time: 15 minutes plus cooling

Cooking time: 35 minutes

Makes 30 biscuits

250g (9oz) whole almonds

4 eggs, plus 2 egg yolks

250g (9oz) caster sugar

pinch of salt

100g (3½oz) extra virgin olive oil

1 tablespoon sweet wine

630g (1lb 6oz) plain flour, plus extra for dusting

2 teaspoons baking powder

2 tablespoons chia seeds

Heat the grill to medium-high. Line two baking trays with baking paper.

Spread the almonds over one of the prepared baking trays in a single layer and place under the grill for 3 minutes until lightly golden. Leave to cool on a wire rack.

Preheat the oven to 200°C (400°F), Gas Mark 6.

Put the eggs, 1 egg yolk, sugar and salt into the bowl of a stand mixer and mix together for 3 minutes until fluffy. Stir in the oil, wine, flour and baking powder and continue to mix to form a smooth, slightly crumbly dough.

Add the almonds and chia seeds to the dough and fold together by hand, then divide the dough into 4 equal-sized pieces. On a clean, floured work surface, roll each dough piece out into a sausage-shaped log approximately 20cm (8 inches) long. Transfer the dough logs to the prepared baking tray and brush with the remaining egg yolk. Bake for 20 minutes until pale gold in colour, then remove from the oven and leave to cool for 30 minutes.

Once the dough logs have cooled, cut them into 2-cm (1-inch) pieces. Rearrange the biscuits on the baking tray and bake in the oven for a further 10 minutes until firm and golden brown.

Leave the biscuits to cool completely on a wire rack before serving. They can be kept, stored in an airtight container, for up to 3 months.

Grissini

BREADSTICKS

Bread is one of the most heartening foods ever; I find it almost healing. So when I visit friends and find breadsticks on the table, I know that behind the scenes is a host with an eye for details. Whether I'm about to sit down to a lavish feast or a simple, everyday meal, I know I'm in for a treat.

For the breadsticks, measure the temperature of the water with a food thermometer if possible, as you need to be quite precise. You can make the dough by hand, with a mixer or in a bread machine. I prefer the latter, simply because I sometimes have an indolent nature.

Preparation time: 20 minutes plus rising

Cooking time: 15 minutes

Makes 30 breadsticks

200ml (1/3 pint) bottled still or filtered water

1 1/2 teaspoons fast-action dried yeast

500g (1lb 2oz) strong white flour

100ml (3 1/2fl oz) extra virgin olive oil

10g (1/4oz) caster sugar or malt extract

15g (1/2oz) fine salt

50g (1 3/4oz) sesame or poppy seeds

Pour the measured water into a pan. Using a food thermometer, check the temperature of the water – it should be 25°C (77°F) – and gently heat it if necessary until it reaches the desired temperature. Pour the water into a large bowl along with the yeast and stir to dissolve. Add 100g (3 1/2oz) of flour and stir everything together to form a wet dough. Leave to rest for 45 minutes.

Once rested, tip the yeast and flour mixture into the bowl of a stand mixer with the dough hook attachment, add the oil, sugar and remaining flour and knead together for 10 minutes to form a firm, elastic dough. Add the salt and knead for a further 3 minutes, then transfer the dough to a bowl, cover with clingfilm and leave to rise in a warm place for 1 hour, or until doubled in size.

Preheat the oven to 160°C (325°F), Gas Mark 3.

Once risen, knock the dough back with your hands and shape into a 60 x 20-cm (23 1/2 x 8-inch) rectangle. Slice the dough lengthways into 2-cm (3/4-inch) thick strips using a sharp knife and roll each strip into a long, unevenly twisted cylinder. Place the breadsticks on a baking tray, spacing them about 1cm (1/2 inch) apart. Sprinkle with the sesame seeds and leave to rest for 15 minutes.

Bake the breadsticks in the oven for 15 minutes until golden brown (be sure to check them often to make sure they don't overcook). Leave to cool on a wire rack, then transfer to an airtight container and store for up to 5 days.

Pangrattato

BREADCRUMBS

I like to mix different odds and ends of bread in my breadcrumbs, to make them more colourful and tasty.

Preparation time: 30 seconds

Makes 400g (14oz)

200g (7oz) stale bread

200g (7oz) stale breadsticks or crackers

1 teaspoon dried sage

Put all the ingredients in a food processor and blend together for 30 seconds or until they become fine breadcrumbs. Store in an airtight container for up to 1 month.

Pesto Romano di zucchine

ROMAN-STYLE COURGETTE PESTO

I'm about to tackle a well-deserved glass of wine when my mother calls: she wants to know if I'm eating enough, sleeping enough, and why I have yet to turn into that perfect little girl. After one of these conversations I'm ravenous. Luckily, my freezer has treats in store for me. I like to spread this pesto on rye bread or dollop some on my *filetto* or pasta, and I'm in heaven.

Preparation time: 10 minutes plus draining

Makes 2 x 250-ml (9fl-oz) jars

2 courgettes

pinch of salt

2 teaspoons dried marjoram

1 garlic clove, peeled and left whole

15 basil leaves

2 tablespoons pine nuts

2 tablespoons extra virgin olive oil

40g (1½oz) pecorino romano cheese

40g (1½oz) Parmesan cheese

Start by sterilizing the jars (*see* page 254).

Slice the ends off the courgettes and discard. Cut the remainder into thin matchsticks. Put the courgette pieces into a colander, place in the sink and sprinkle over a pinch of salt. Leave for 30 minutes to drain away any excess moisture.

Once drained, tip the courgette pieces into a food processor with the marjoram, garlic, basil, pine nuts, oil, pecorino and Parmesan and blend to a smooth, creamy paste. Spoon the pesto into sterilized jam jars and refrigerate for up to 1 week, or transfer to a suitable container and freeze for up to 2 months.

Crostini

CROUTONS

Bread is sacred in Italy, and by that I mean you should never throw it away, as it could make a precious addition to numerous soups and salads. For this recipe, any stale bread will do.

Preparation time: 1 minute

Cooking time: 5 minutes

slices of stale bread

Cut the bread into 1cm (½ inch) cubes and toast them in a non-stick frying pan for about 5 minutes, stirring from time to time, until they are golden and browned at the edges.

Conserva alla cipolla rossa

RED ONION PRESERVE

Someone once told me a story set in Ancient Rome in which undiluted wine caught fire when it came too close to a lit candle. The wine back then was much higher in alcohol and couldn't possibly be drunk without being watered down first, though even today you can still find many people – especially those belonging to the older generation – pouring some water into their glass of red. I like to mix together my favourite leftover wine with sweet, burgundy-coloured onions to make this preserve, the perfect accompaniment to a roast as well as all kinds of cheeses (see photograph overleaf). Beware, though, once you open the jar the onion preserve should be stored in the fridge and consumed within a week.

Preparation time: 5 minutes plus macerating

Cooking time: 30 minutes

Makes 6 x 250-ml (9fl-oz) jars

1.5kg (3lb 5oz) large red onions, peeled, halved and thinly sliced

175g (7oz) caster sugar

175g (7oz) light brown sugar

150ml (¼ pint) rosé wine

50ml (2fl oz) red wine vinegar

4 garlic cloves

2 kaffir lime leaves

Start by sterilizing the jars (*see* page 254).

Put all the ingredients into a large bowl. Stir well, cover with clingfilm and leave to macerate for at least 8 hours, preferably overnight.

When you're ready to cook, remove and discard the lime leaves from the softened onions and tip everything into a large casserole dish. Bring to a gentle simmer and cook over a low heat for 30 minutes, stirring occasionally, until the onions are soft and sticky and the mixture is thick and jam-like in consistency.

To check that the preserve is ready, apply the following test: place a small plate in the freezer for 10 minutes, then pour a few drops of the onion liquid onto the cold saucer. After a minute, run your finger through the drops – if the preserve wrinkles slightly, it's good to go. If it doesn't, return the pan to the heat and simmer for a further 2–3 minutes, then test again.

Spoon the warm onion preserve into sterilized jars, seal tightly and store in a dry place away from sunlight for up to 6 months.

Marmellata di uva e noci pecan

GRAPE & PECAN JAM

The history of jam starts with melancholy. Catherine of Aragon, the unlucky first wife of
Henry VIII, was said to have missed the fruits of her homeland so much that she had jams
made and shipped to her from Spain to England.

Like the tan lines from your swimsuit, preserved fruit reminds us of carefree summer days
as the autumn leaves start to fall. This grape and pecan jam makes a lovely change from the
usual, and works a treat spread on top of sweet melba toasts (*see* page 35).

Preparation time: 20 minutes plus
macerating

Cooking time: 1 hour

Makes 4 x 250ml (9fl-oz) jars

1kg (2lb 4oz) red seedless grapes,
  halved

2 lemons, halved and thinly sliced

500g (1lb 2oz) caster sugar

100g (3½oz) pecan nut halves

4 tablespoons brandy or cognac

Put the grape halves and lemon slices in a large bowl, pour over the sugar
and leave to macerate for 3 hours, until the juices start to run.

Remove the lemon slices from the bowl and discard. then tip the rest of the
mixture into a large saucepan. Bring to a simmer over a low heat and cook
for 1 hour, stirring frequently.

Meanwhile, sterilize the jars. Preheat the oven to 120°C (250°F), Gas
Mark ½. Wash the jars and their lids in hot, soapy water, rinse thoroughly
and place in the oven for 10 minutes to dry completely.

To check that the jam is ready, apply the following test: place a small plate
in the freezer for 10 minutes, then pour a drop of jam onto the cold saucer.
Leave it for a minute, then flip the saucer upside down – if the jam stays
firmly attached to the saucer and doesn't fall, then it's good to go. If it
doesn't, carry on simmering for 2–3 minutes, then test again.

Once ready, remove the jam from the heat and leave to cool for 5 minutes,
then gently stir in the nuts and liqueur.

Pour the hot jam into the sterilized jars and screw the caps on firmly to
close. Turn the jars upside down to cool for 45 minutes, then flip them
over. Store in the cupboard or pantry for up to 6 months.

Cubetti di ghiaccio

HANDMADE ICE CUBES

Gracefully clinking in glasses, ice cubes can be so much more than simply functional.
To emphasize their power of suggestion and add a hint of colour to my drinks, I like to enrich
mine with all kinds of fruits, juices and herbs. Are you planning to offer a fruity refreshment?
Instead of water, just fill your ice cube trays with the fruit juice of your choice, pop them in
the freezer and forget about them, until the next party. May the sun be with you.

Preparation time: 5 minutes plus freezing

Makes one regular ice cube tray's worth

4 red grapes

1/4 kiwi, peeled

1 redcurrant stalk

8 mint leaves, halved

150ml (1/4 pint) water or fresh fruit juice

Cut each grape in half and the kiwi into 3-mm (1/8-inch) cubes. Strip the redcurrants from the stalk.

Fill half the moulds of an ice cube tray with the grape halves, kiwi pieces and redcurrants, keeping the fruits separate. Top each mould with half a mint leaf and fill with water or juice. Freeze until solid (this will take at least 5 hours) and keep for up to 6 months.

Il Negroni

NEGRONI COCKTAIL

The Negroni can be 'right' or 'wrong'. Either way, this bitter, candy-apple red aperitif is extremely soothing and relieves all kinds of post-work stress. The secret to its brilliant colour? Cochineal, a scarlet dye now used primarily for colouring food that was once used by our grandmothers to dye wool or cotton.

The alternative version of this cocktail, the 'wrong' one, is not wrong at all and is actually quite good – known also as the *negroni sbagliato*, here prosecco is used instead of gin, making it much lighter. I like to add a hint of homemade Roman-style Sambuca (*see* page 271) and some Handmade Ice Cubes (*see* page 266) to make my Negronis. Fresh and vibrant, these cocktails are an impeccable way to get the party started. The recipe listed below calls for double servings and high spirits.

Preparation time: 5 minutes plus chilling

Serves 4

4 Handmade Ice Cubes (*see* page 266) or regular ice cubes, crushed

240ml (8½fl oz) gin or prosecco

240ml (8½fl oz) red vermouth

240ml (8½fl oz) Campari or Gran Classico

4 dashes of Roman-style Sambuca (*see* page 271) or regular sambuca

4 orange twists, to garnish

Place 4 martini glasses in the freezer to chill for 10 minutes.

Line up the chilled glasses on a work surface and add crushed ice to each. Pour a quarter of the gin or prosecco, vermouth and Campari or Gran Classico into each glass and finish with a dash of sambuca. Stir together, garnish with the orange twists and serve.

Sambuca alla Romana

ROMAN-STYLE SAMBUCA

Some types of cooking are therapeutic, time spent in joyful activity. Other culinary processes, such as the one involved in making a liqueur, for example, resemble a propitiatory ritual. Here night-sky dark star anise, bronze cinnamon and a hint of coriander make up the ingredients of this famous liqueur, which is also used in the making of Tarallucci al Vino (*see* page 43). Sooner or later, everyone in Rome drinks it, often dropping a couple of roasted coffee beans in the glass for extra aroma. After all that food, you need a little bitterness to prepare you for the next banquet. And leave you happily oblivious, of course.

Preparation time: 10 minutes plus 23 days storing

Makes 2 x 1-litre (1¾-pint) bottles

80g (3oz) star anise

1 teaspoon coriander seeds

1 cinnamon stick

4 cloves

1 vanilla pod

1 lemon

700ml (1¼pints) eau-de-vie (colourless fruit liqueur), 40–80% proof

500g (1lb 2oz) caster sugar

1 litre (1¾ pints) water

Place the star anise, coriander seeds, cinnamon stick, cloves, vanilla pod and lemon in a 2-litre (3½-pint) Kilner jar, pour over the eau-de-vie and seal tightly. Store for 20 days in a dark, dry place, giving the jar a shake every other day to allow all the ingredients to mingle together.

After the 20 days are up, dissolve the sugar in the measured water and add to the jar. Close the jar and leave for a further 3 days, then strain the liqueur into clean, dry bottles. Enjoy immediately or store for up to 2 years.

Chapter II
MIDNIGHT MUNCHIES

These days, Via dei Coronari, the road of the crown makers, is home to the most exclusive antique shops and jewellers. Not far from here, you will find La Casa di Fiammetta, once the home of Cesare Borgia's mistress. Right around the corner, Via del Governo Vecchio is the road of the old government. Once dominated by the unrivalled supremacy of the Pope, the street now boasts an undisputedly great *osteria*, Da Tonino, serving *straccetti* (*see* page 279) and *fusilli aglio e olio* (*see* page 290). Pontiffs have travelled the length of Via del Governo Vecchio for centuries, sitting on a ceremonial throne carried on the shoulders of the offspring of Rome's A-listers, next in line for power. These young men would often crack jokes at the expense of their passenger, who would amiably punish them by sending them to the fortified Castel S. Angelo, the papal jail, for a few days of isolated contemplation with room service.

Somewhere on this awfully charming road, you might bump into Dolores. This local legend – her green eyes glowing like a Sgroppino (*see* page 295) as she tells you about her adventures working as an extra for Federico Fellini – now sleeps under the stars. Some say she once possessed a fortune in precious jewels and other gifts from her lovers, others talk about her addiction to lust and Affogato al Caffè (*see* page 293). Did she ever really work with the director of *La Dolce Vita*? Despite her bruised appearance today, you might still find a glance of past glory in her sneaky smile... maybe.

The first 'talking statue' of Rome, Pasquino gave voice to those who would find it too transgressive or hazardous to share their discontent with state or church in public, in the days before freedom of speech for all. Women and men of all kinds came to the ruined Greek statue on the corner of Piazza Pasquino, their heads covered by black veils. Complaints and protests would appear on the statue in the form of satirical poems, styled with wit, subtlety and a huge amount of derision. Public figures were caricatured in words: some were transformed into monuments, some into animals, some even into Carciofi alla Romana (see *page* 283). Dishes of Rome styled up for all kitchens.

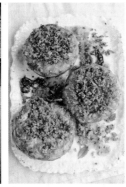

Grattachecca

ROMAN GRANITA

To me, there's nothing more emblematic of the torrid Roman summer than this ice-cold dessert: it's only when the *grattachecca* kiosks open again that I know the time of eternal flirtation and sunburn has arrived. A day trip to the coastal town of Sperlonga, home of the grotto of Tiberius and some seriously amazing mozzarella, wouldn't be the same if it didn't end, after the inevitable traffic jam on the way back to Rome, with a visit to Alla Fonte d'Oro, the oldest *grattacheccaro* in Trastevere. There are two occasions on which I like to consume this granita: when it's so hot that your internal thermometer is rendered useless, and when spring is in full blossom, allowing you to regain your grasp on the flavours of the warmer seasons, lost during the winter. Here is an easy do-it-yourself version.

Preparation time: 5 minutes plus cooling

Cooking time: 5 minutes

Serves 4

250g (9oz) strawberries, hulled and halved, or other berries

2 tablespoons lemon juice

50g (1¾oz) icing sugar

30 ice cubes

60g (2¼oz) coconut chunks, banana slices or other fruit pieces, to decorate

small handful of mint leaves

Gently heat the strawberries in a small non-stick frying pan for 3 minutes until they have softened and collapsed. Using a potato masher, crush the strawberries into a thick paste. Whisk in the lemon juice and sugar and simmer for a further 3 minutes until everything has reduced down to a syrup. Sieve the syrup into a bowl and transfer to the refrigerator. Leave to cool for 1 hour.

When ready to serve, take the ice out of the freezer and place in a large sealable freezer bag. Using a rolling pin or ice crusher, if you have one, smash the ice to a slushy consistency.

Divide the crushed ice between 4 glasses. Pour over the fruit syrup and stir together with a cocktail spoon. Decorate with coconut chunks, banana slices or fruit chunks of your choice, and finish with a few mint leaves.

SHALLOW-FRIED CHEESE & EGG BALLS

This is a dish made of simple ingredients, found in all Roman homes, but I think this general rule can also be extended in some form to this book's lovely readers – I assume we all have some leftover soft cheese in the fridge, waiting to be put to good use. There's something unmistakably honest about eating leftovers, maybe because the cook's good intentions have been applied to the ingredients for a second time, and most eloquently, too. The added egg helps bind together all the other ingredients, as it does in so many recipes. These balls don't take long to prepare: once they've browned in the hot oil, they can be considered done.

Preparation time: 10 minutes

Cooking time: 20 minutes

Makes 20 *pallotte*

120ml (4fl oz) milk

150g (5½oz) stale bread, torn into small pieces

250g (9oz) ricotta, cottage cheese or other mild, soft cheese

1 large egg

handful of flat-leaf parsley leaves, chopped

2 teaspoons salt

2 garlic cloves, thinly sliced

130ml (4fl oz) vegetable or olive oil

1 x 250-g (9-oz) can cherry tomatoes

¼ teaspoon caster sugar

handful of basil leaves, chopped, plus extra to garnish

1 teaspoon pink peppercorns

Pour the milk into a small bowl, add the bread pieces and soak briefly.

Squeeze any excess milk out of the bread, then tip it into a bowl with the cheese, egg, parsley, salt and half the sliced garlic. Using your hands, mix everything together well, then roll the mixture into walnut-sized balls.

Heat 2 tablespoons of oil in a frying pan, add the tomatoes, sugar, chopped basil and remaining garlic. Season with salt, bring to a simmer and cook for 10 minutes until the sauce has thickened and reduced slightly.

Meanwhile, heat the remaining 100ml (3½fl oz) vegetable oil in a large non-stick frying pan over a medium heat until hot. Carefully lower the cheese and egg balls into the oil and fry for 5 minutes until golden brown. Lift the balls out of the frying pan using a slotted spoon and place them on a dish covered with kitchen paper to drain off any excess oil.

Carefully add the fried balls to the sauce and cook for a further 2–3 minutes to warm through, then transfer to a serving platter and scatter over the pink peppercorns and a few whole basil leaves to garnish. Enjoy.

Straccetti al Marsala accompagnati da spinaci e pane raffermo

SLICED VEAL WITH MARSALA ACCOMPANIED BY SPINACH & STALE BREAD

A paparazzo is a photographer whose job it is to capture the rich and famous in the most compromising situations. The word was used for the first time in Fellini's *La Dolce Vita,* for a slimy and persistent character who strolls around Rome eager to take unofficial pictures in order to gain fame or (better still) infamy. Many celebrities have fought the invasive nature of the paparazzi with explosive public outbursts, while some have made the photographers promise to tear their worst pictures into strips. The original version of this dish calls for beef, but you can use any kind of meat. Just reduce it to strips and you'll have your *straccetti* sorted. As simple as taking a picture.

Preparation time: 10 minutes

Cooking time: 20 minutes

Serves 6

80g (3oz) plain flour

1 teaspoon ground turmeric

600g (1lb 5oz) organic veal or pork escalopes, cut into 1-cm (¹/₂-inch) slices

3 tablespoons extra virgin olive oil

knob of unsalted butter

6 tablespoons Marsala wine

a drop of soy sauce

2 tablespoons cornflour mixed together with 130ml (4¹/₂fl oz) water

Spinach:

500g (1lb 2oz) spinach leaves

150g (5¹/₂oz) stale bread, cut into 1-cm (¹/₂-inch) cubes

80g (3oz) pancetta cubes

1 garlic clove, peeled and left whole

2 tablespoons extra virgin olive oil

2 tablespoons grated pecorino romano cheese

salt

Place the flour and turmeric in a plastic food bag, add the veal slices, seal the bag and shake to coat.

Heat the oil and butter together in a large frying pan over a medium heat. Add the coated meat pieces and cook, stirring occasionally, for 5 minutes until lightly golden on each side. Remove the meat from the pan and set aside.

Pour the Marsala, soy sauce and cornflour solution into the pan, bring to a simmer and leave to bubble away for 5 minutes until thickened and reduced.

While the sauce is reducing, cook the spinach. Put the spinach leaves in a large saucepan and pour over just enough boiling water to cover. Season with salt, bring to a simmer and cook over a medium heat for 5 minutes, then add the bread and stir everything together well to allow it to soak up the cooking liquid. Tip the mixture into a colander to drain off any excess liquid, then return it to the pan and mash everything together roughly with a fork or potato masher.

Heat a small non-stick frying pan over a low heat, add the pancetta and fry for 2–3 minutes, until the pancetta has rendered some of its fat. Add the garlic and cook for a further 3 minutes until the pancetta is crisp and golden, then tip the garlic and pancetta into the mashed spinach and mix together well. Stir in the olive oil and season with salt to taste.

Return the veal pieces to the sauce and warm through for 1–2 minutes, then divide between plates. Sprinkle the grated pecorino over the spinach and serve.

Carciofi alla Romana

ROMAN STYLE BRAISED ARTICHOKES

Behind the Circus Maximus, among the marvels of the Palatine ruins, there's a rose garden comprising more than 1,100 rose varieties. I'm surprised that no artichokes grow here, because to me this is the vegetable most reminiscent of the most romantic flower of them all. Not only is it fragrantly delicious at first bite, its aftertaste is just heavenly. When artichokes are in season, Romans eat them like a panacea for all life's worries. The good news is that they are low in calories and make a terrific liver cleanser. Hearty and fulfilling. Rejoice. These artichokes will keep in the refrigerator for up to five days and are excellent added to pasta or served alongside poached eggs.

Preparation time: 15 minutes

Cooking time: 40 minutes

Serves 4

large handful of mint leaves

2 kaffir lime leaves, finely chopped

1 garlic clove, finely chopped

100g (3½oz) breadcrumbs (*see* page 262)

3 tablespoons extra virgin olive oil

4 long-stemmed artichokes, cleaned (see page 13) and placed in acidulated water

150ml (¼ pint) vegetable stock

salt

Finely chop half the mint and put it in a bowl with the lime leaves, garlic, breadcrumbs and 1 tablespoon of the extra virgin olive oil. Season with salt and mix together well.

Delicately pry open the cavity of each prepared artichoke with a teaspoon and fill with 4 teaspoons of the herb mixture.

Gently heat the remaining 2 tablespoons of olive oil in a large saucepan. Add the artichokes to the pan stem-side up and pour over the vegetable stock.

Scatter over the remaining mint leaves, bring to a simmer and cook over a medium-low heat, covered, for 40 minutes, until the thickest part of the artichoke stem is tender to the point of a sharp knife.

Season the artichokes with salt to taste and transfer to a serving dish. Serve hot or, for best results, leave to cool to room temperature before serving.

Salsiccia con lenticchie, porro e finocchio

BRAISED SAUSAGES WITH LENTILS, LEEKS & FENNEL

I can't get enough of these nutty legumes, which are considered a symbol of good luck in Italy and are so easily matched with a large range of ingredients. They make a wonderful addition to stews, soups and salads, and they're also a great meat substitute. There's a salami in Italy called *finocchiona* – it's one of those foods that lift you up no matter what life throws at you. It's more of a countryside delicacy, not available all year round or easy to find, but I like to re-create its smells and flavours in my own kitchen with this one-pot supper, to be devoured on the couch in front of your favourite old movie.

Preparation time: 5 minutes

Cooking time: 30 minutes

Serves 4

4 tablespoons extra virgin olive oil

1 leek, trimmed, cleaned and finely sliced lengthways

1 fennel bulb, trimmed and cut into rough strips

400g (14oz) pork sausages

250g (9oz) Castelluccio or Puy lentils

350ml (12fl oz) vegetable stock

10g (1/4oz) fennel seeds

small handful of chives, chopped

salt and pepper

Warm the oil in a frying pan over a medium heat, add the leek and fry for 5 minutes until softened and translucent. Add the fennel and sausages and cook for a further 5 minutes until the sausages are browned on all sides.

Add the lentils to the pan and pour over the stock. Bring to a boil, then reduce the heat to a gentle simmer and leave to cook for 25 minutes, or until the lentils have softened and the sausages are cooked through. Season with salt and pepper to taste.

Divide the lentils and sausages between plates and scatter over the fennel seeds and chopped chives to finish. Serve.

Saltimbocca alla Romana con pera caramellata, salvia fritta e lattuga brasata

ROMAN-STYLE SALTIMBOCCA WITH CARAMELIZED PEAR, FRIED SAGE & BRAISED LETTUCE

Preparation time: 25 minutes

Cooking time: 40 minutes

Serves 4

100g (3½oz) unsalted butter

1 tablespoon caster sugar

10 sage leaves, 2 finely chopped and 8 left whole

½ William pear, peeled, cored and cut into small chunks

8 x 70-g (2½-oz) organic veal escalopes, trimmed

30g (1oz) plain flour

4 x 10-g (¼-oz) prosciutto slices, halved

150ml (¼ pint) white wine

Braised lettuce:

500g (1lb 2oz) lettuce, trimmed and leaves separated

1 carrot, cut into 1-cm (½-inch) cubes

1 large white onion, cut into 1-cm (½-inch) cubes

3 tablespoons extra virgin olive oil

1 teaspoon chopped thyme leaves

1 teaspoon chopped tarragon leaves

1 teaspoon chopped flat-leaf parsley leaves

200ml (⅓ pint) vegetable stock

Fried sage:

1 tablespoon plain flour

50ml (2fl oz) sparkling water

50ml (2fl oz) extra virgin olive oil

3 salted anchovies, rinsed and cut into 1-cm (½-inch) pieces

25 sage leaves

As challenging or cheerful as my day may have been, when night-time comes, wherever in the world I might be, I make my way to the kitchen. This way, I'll always be at home. For this recipe, you'll need to pound the meat for it to really melt in the mouth. If you don't have a meat mallet, take a heavy frying pan, cover your meat with clingfilm, and bash away. It's also a great way to relieve the stress of a working day.

Preheat the oven to 200°C (400°F), Gas Mark 6.

For the braised lettuce, bring a large saucepan of salted water to a boil, add the lettuce leaves and blanch for 3 minutes. Drain the lettuce well and rinse under cold running water, then put into a baking dish along with the carrot and onion pieces. Drizzle over the oil, scatter over the chopped herbs and mix together well, then pour over the stock. Cover with baking paper and cook in the oven for 30 minutes, or until all the stock has been absorbed and the vegetables are soft and tender.

While the lettuce is cooking, prepare the *saltimbocca*. Melt half the butter in a small saucepan over a low heat. Add the sugar, chopped sage leaves and pear to the pan and cook for 10 minutes, or until the pear chunks are tender but still holding their shape. Remove from the heat and set aside.

Bash the veal pieces out as thinly and evenly as possible (see above), then dust with the flour, shaking off the excess. Spoon a teaspoon of the pear mixture into the centre of a veal piece and press a piece of prosciutto on top to create a parcel. Top the prosciutto with a sage leaf and skewer with a toothpick to fix everything in place. Repeat with the remaining ingredients.

Gently heat the remaining butter in a large frying pan. Add the veal, prosciutto-side down, and cook for 2 minutes on each side, turning carefully, until golden (you may need to do this in batches). Remove the veal escalopes and transfer to a low oven to keep warm. Add the white wine to the pan and bring to a boil over a high heat. Season with salt and pepper and reduce until syrupy.

For the fried sage, mix together the flour, water and a pinch of salt to form a batter. Heat the olive oil in a frying pan. Sandwich the anchovy pieces between the sage leaves, dip them in the batter and fry for about 1 minute per side, until golden brown. Drain the crispy sage leaves on kitchen paper and scatter over the saltimbocca. Serve with the braised lettuce.

Pappa al pomodoro

BREAD & TOMATO SOUP

'*Viva la Pappa col Pomodoro*' is a popular tune sung by Rita Pavone, a teen star back in the Sixties. As well as singing about this dish, she also played the title character in one of Italy's first ever TV series, *Il Giornalino di Gian Burrasca* – a boy whose name translates as 'Johnny Tempest'. This nickname, which the boy was given by his family because of his bad behaviour (more a matter of exuberance than malice), has since become proverbial, and is now given to any unruly kid. Bread and tomato, the quintessential Italian combination that never goes wrong, even if all else does.

Preparation time: 20 minutes

Cooking time: 25 minutes

Serves 4

3 tablespoons extra virgin olive oil

1 spring onion, finely chopped

400g (14oz) cherry vine tomatoes, halved

large handful of basil leaves, roughly chopped

1 teaspoon ground nutmeg

120ml (4fl oz) vegetable stock

1 round crusty sourdough loaf or 4 crusty bread rolls

1 garlic clove, peeled and cut in half

pinch of chilli flakes

zest of 1 lemon

basil leaves, to garnish

salt

Gently heat 2 tablespoons of olive oil in a frying pan, add the spring onion and leave to cook over a low heat, stirring occasionally, for 5 minutes until softened and lightly golden.

Add the tomatoes, chopped basil and nutmeg and cook, stirring, for 10 minutes. Pour over the stock, bring to a gentle simmer and cook for a further 10 minutes until everything has reduced to a thick sauce.

Cut the top off the loaf of bread or each bread roll , if using, and carefully scoop out the insides to form a bread 'bowl', being careful to keep the crust intact. Rub the removed bread with the garlic halves, tear it into thumb-sized pieces and toast it for 3 minutes in a dry frying pan over a medium heat.

Tip the toasted bread pieces into the tomato sauce and season with salt. Sprinkle over the chilli flakes, then stir everything together until thick and silky in texture. Remove from the heat, drizzle over the remaining 1 tablespoon of olive oil and spoon the soup into the loaf or bread rolls. Sprinkle over the lemon zest and some basil leaves and serve.

Fusilli lunghi aglio, olio, indivia, peperoncino, capperi e molliche

FUSILLI PASTA WITH GARLIC, OLIVE OIL, ENDIVE, CHILLIES, CAPERS & BREADCRUMBS

This plain and extremely simple Roman dish is one of the first things Italian kids attempt to cook. The name of the recipe itself echoes with the far-from-perfect Roman dialect: *'aio, oio e peperoncino'*, which is how we are all used to hearing it pronounced. I like to give this dish a Roman look with a little of my own style, of course. *Colatura di alici* is the amber-coloured, aromatic juice of salted anchovies. It can be difficult to find, so to replace it, I cook some anchovies in the most exquisite extra virgin olive oil I can find. A long spiral-shaped type of pasta like fusilli lunghi is perfect for this sauce, but any long pasta shape will do.

Preparation time: 10 minutes

Cooking time: 10 minutes

Serves 4

350g (12oz) fusilli lunghi or linguine pasta

8 tablespoons extra virgin olive oil

2 garlic cloves, peeled and left whole

4 anchovies in olive oil

2 endive or chicory heads, trimmed and finely sliced

1 teaspoon chopped red chilli or chilli flakes

1 teaspoon salted capers, rinsed

large handful of flat-leaf parsley leaves, finely chopped, plus extra to garnish

20g (³/₄oz) unsalted butter

50g (1³/₄oz) stale bread, cut into 1-cm (¹/₂-inch) cubes, to garnish

salt

Bring a large saucepan of salted water to a boil. Add the pasta and cook according to the packet instructions until al dente.

While the pasta is cooking, prepare the sauce. Gently heat the olive oil in a large non-stick frying pan with the garlic and anchovies, stirring occasionally, until the anchovies have dissolved. Stir in the endive, chilli and capers.

Once cooked, drain the pasta, reserving a ladleful of the cooking water. Tip the pasta into the sauce, add the parsley, butter and pasta cooking water and stir everything together well.

Divide the pasta between bowls and scatter over the bread cubes – which you could quickly toast in a non-stick frying pan first, for extra crunchiness – and a little extra chopped parsley to garnish. Serve.

Affogato al caffè

ICE-CREAM DROWNED IN COFFEE

This traditional recipe, typical of the Italian summer, combines two classics of Italian gastronomy – artisanal gelato and coffee. In Italy we all make coffee with a moka pot, but other methods are fine: it's a dense and bitter espresso-type coffee you're after. Below I'm offering you a recipe for fuss-free homemade gelato, but if you want to go for shop-bought ice cream, the flavours that are best suited to being drowned in coffee are vanilla, *stracciatella* and the nutty ones, like praline. Avoid fruity flavours as they don't work well with coffee. Remember, the scoop of gelato for each serving needs to be appropriately indulgent.

Preparation time: 10 minutes plus freezing

Cooking time: 5 minutes

Serves 4

4 shots hot good-quality espresso coffee

4 teaspoons caster sugar

50g (1¾oz) unsalted pistachios, crushed

Homemade gelato:

350ml (12fl oz) milk

50g (1¾oz) caster sugar

100g (3½oz) hazelnuts

For the homemade gelato, pour the milk into an ice cube tray, place in the freezer and leave to freeze until solid (this will take at least 5 hours).

When the frozen milk is ready, make up the espressos and sweeten them with the sugar while still hot. Set aside to cool for 10 minutes.

In a food processor, mix the sugar and hazelnuts together to a fine powder. Add the frozen milk and blend together for a few seconds until you get an ice cream consistency – the time varies depending on the machine you're using, so watch this closely.

Scoop the ice cream into 4 glasses and pour the coffee around each (if you pour the coffee directly on top, the ice cream will melt and it will spoil the presentation). Sprinkle over the crushed pistachios and enjoy immediately.

Sgroppino

FROTHY LEMON SORBET

In Italy, when people talk about finishing a lavish meal, you will often hear comments like: 'We had fruit, dessert, coffee and coffee killers.' Coffee killers often come in the form of dessert wines or liqueurs and this is the category you would also put *sgroppino* in, though it has a lighter feel to it and a lower alcohol content than most. If you have never tasted this citrusy delicacy before, then I strongly suggest you do so. And if you have, forget about all the rules and follow this ridiculously easy recipe for a glorious end to a meal. I like to serve this sorbet in vintage champagne glasses. Also, I would recommend that you have a little extra on hand, because this surely calls for seconds and thirds and...

Preparation time: 5 minutes

Serves 4

8 tablespoons lemon ice cream

approx. 400ml (14fl oz) prosecco

2 teaspoons ground nutmeg

1 teaspoon freshly ground black pepper

zest of 1 lemon, to garnish

Place the ice cream in a large bowl and beat it with a balloon whisk for 1–2 minutes to soften it up slightly. Gradually add the prosecco, continuing to whisk, until the mixture is light, creamy and fluffy in consistency. Whisk in the nutmeg and pepper, pour the *sgroppino* into champagne glasses and sprinkle over the lemon zest to garnish. Enjoy immediately.

INDEX

A

agretti tart, with beef rolls 98–101
almonds
    cantucci biscuit & sweet wine
        semifreddo 236–7
    Tuscan tozzetti biscuits 257
Amatriciana sauce 193
anchovies 12
    in aubergine boats 84
    on bruschette 46–7
    Christmas fish 222
    dressing 120
    fried sage 287
    marinated 147
    mozzarella in a carriage 130–1
    tomato & ricotta ravioli 168
    in tuna sauce 118
aperitivo 127–49
apple
    chestnut & hazelnut cake with
        candied oranges 244
    parsnip & beetroot salad 183
    in polenta cake 58–9
artichokes
    with maccheroni, courgettes &
        ricotta salata 192
    in oil 252–3
    parmigiana, with beef 108–9
    preparing 13
    Roman-style braised 282–3
    in savoury pie 50
    in vignarola 157
asparagus, in baked pasta 102–3
aubergine 46–7, 84–5
avocado 72–3, 172–3

B

banana, chocolate, amaretti & tutti
    frutti cake 233
beans, broad 104–5, 157
beans, cannellini 158
beans, haricot 196
beans, runner 96–7
beef
    Ascoli-style stuffed olives 137
    in meatballs 117
    mini meat loaves 134–6
    ribollita soup 196
    rolls with agretti tart 98–101
    stew with artichoke parmigiana
        108–9
beetroot, parsnip & apple salad 183

Bel Paese cheese 98, 145
biscuits
    dunking 32–3
    shortbread trio with jam 57
    Tuscan tozzetti, with chia seeds
        256–7
    ugly but good 26–7
blackberries 228–9, 237, 242
bocconcini 120
bomboloni 31
bread
    breadcrumbs 262
    breadsticks 258–9
    brioche with chocolate 24–5
    bruschette, three kinds 46–7
    croutons 263
    Easter 207, 211
    fried cheese & egg balls 278
    greased, with pork chops 182–3
    Imperial-style golden, with
        clementine jelly 212–15
    mozzarella in a carriage 130–1
    mozzarella 'sandwich' 71
    rosetta loaf with mortadella,
        stracchino & mostarda 68–70
    salad 132–3
    sandwich wheels with prosciutto
        mousse 56
    & spinach with veal 279
    sweet Melba toast 34–5
    tea sandwiches (*tramezzini*) 146
    & tomato soup 288–9
breakfast 15–37
brioche, with chocolate 24–5
broad beans
    & pecorino mousse with salmon
        104–5
    in vignarola 157
broccoli 46–7, 168
bruschette, three kinds 46–7
bucatini
    with Amatriciana sauce 193
    with clams & minty potatoes
        154–5
buns, sticky 18–19
butter 13

C

cabbage 74, 196
cake 225–48
    apple, chestnut & hazelnut with
        candied oranges 244

chestnut flour 245
chocolate, amaretti & tutti frutti
    232–3
pineapple mimosa, with candied
    flowers 204–6
polenta, with pumpkin &
    apple 58–9
sour cherry & ricotta roll 246–7
wheat & candied fruit 60–1
candied flowers 204–6
candied fruit 60–1
cannelloni, ricotta & saffron 121–3
cantucci biscuits 237
capers 72, 84, 112, 118, 149, 154, 290
cappelletti pasta cake with cream,
    ham, liver & peas 114–15
cardoons 164
Carnival, sweet dough balls 223
carpaccio, sea bass, with peaches,
    kiwi & rocket 75–7
castagnole 223
cauliflower 164, 196
cavolo nero, ribollita soup 196
celery
    in bread salad 132–3
    pesto 124
chard 51–3, 196
Cheddar cheese
    artichoke parmigiana 109
    in baked pasta 103
    in courgette boats 84
cheese *see* types of cheese
cherries
    chocolate, amaretti & tutti frutti
        cake 233
    ice cream fruits 228–9
    sour cherry & ricotta roll cake
        246–7
chestnuts
    apple & hazelnut cake 244
    & cauliflower, with lamb cutlets
        164
    chestnut flour cake 245
chia seeds 257
chicken
    Ascoli-style stuffed olives 137
    galantine with cheesy grapes
        142–3
    livers 114
    mini meat loaves 134–6
    in penne gratin 171
    Roman-style, with peppers 178–9

salad with spelt, courgettes &
goats' cheese 44–5
stew with artichoke parmigiana
108–9
in white soup 125
chickpeas 88–9, 158–9
chicory
in agretti tart 98–9
with fusilli pasta 290
puntarelle salad 120
ricotta & saffron cannelloni 121–3
sautéed 112
chocolate
amaretti & tutti frutti cake 232–3
& ricotta Ghetto-style pie 240
Christmas fish 222
clams, with bucatini 154–5
clementine jelly 212, 213
coconut & ricotta balls 202–3
cod, with chickpeas 88–9
coffee, with ice cream 292–3
conchiglioni, stuffed 72–3
cotechino, with fennel, olive, orange
& pomegranate salad 218–21
courgettes
& aubergine boats 84–5
with maccheroni, artichokes
& ricotta salata 192
Roman-style pesto 262
spelt salad with chicken & goats'
cheese 44–5
stuffed flowers 138–9
cream cheese 142, 146
cream puffs, St Joseph's Day 30
croquettes, potato 134–6
croutons 263
cucumber 132–3, 183
custard pie 238–9

D
doughnuts, baked 31
drinks
frothy lemon sorbet 294–5
negroni cocktail 268–9
Roman-style sambuca 270–1

E
Easter bread
with eggs 207
with pecorino, honey & salami
210–11
edamame, in vignarola 157
eel & bay leaf skewers with
horseradish sauce 170
eggs
cooking with 12
spaghetti omelette 78–9
in tuna cream 149

F
fans, flaky pastry 20–1
fennel
with citrusy monkfish 96–7
lentils & leeks with sausages 284
sea bass carpaccio 75
figs 212, 228–9
flowers, candied 204–6
Fontina cheese
in baked pasta 103
in filled beef rolls 98
& sausage polenta sandwich 145
stuffed courgette flowers 138–9
in suppli 136
friar's beard 98
fritters, three kinds 134–6

G
gnocchi
ricotta, with prawns & pistachios
86–7
semolina, with pork rib sauce
94–5
goats' cheese, spelt salad with
chicken & courgettes 44–5
gorgonzola cheese 142
granita 276–7
granola 22–3
grapes
cheesy 142–3
ice cubes 266
& pecan jam 265–6
with stewed rabbit & olives 194
guanciale 192, 193

H
haddock, with chickpeas 88–9
ham
in capelletti pasta cake 114
in courgette boats 84
sandwich wheels with prosciutto
mousse 56
in savoury pie with artichokes
& peas 50
see also mortadella; prosciutto
hazelnuts 244
herbs
in ice cubes 266
using 12
horseradish sauce 170

I
ice cream 228–9, 292–3
ice cubes 266–7, 276–7
ingredients, staples 12–13

J
jelly, clementine 212, 213

K
kale, in ribollita soup 196
kiwi 75–7, 266

L
lamb, crispy cutlets with cauliflower
& chestnuts 165–7
lardo 124, 158
leeks
in baked asparagus 103
lentils & fennel with sausages 284
in vegetable pie 51
leftovers 71, 79, 98, 175, 196
lemon sole, & rice timbale with
prosecco gravy 184–5
lemons
filled with tuna cream 148–9
frothy lemon sorbet 294–5
tiramisù 241–3
lentils, with sausages 284–5
lettuce
braised 287
sautéed 112
in vignarola 157

M
maccheroni pasta, with artichokes,
courgettes & ricotta salata 192
mango 96
maritozzi 18–19
mascarpone cheese 149, 241
meat loaves, mini 134–6
meatballs 116–17
merende 39–61
meringue, with orange sauce 230–1
mimosa cake, pineapple, with
candied flowers 204–6
monkfish
with chickpeas 88–9
citrus & fennel, with runner beans
96–7
mortadella
cabbage veal bundles 74
in chicken galantine 142
with rosetta loaf 69
mostarda 69
mozzarella cheese
artichoke parmigiana 109
bocconcini 120
in a carriage 130–1
mini pizzas 55
in potato croquettes 136
'sandwich' 71
in savoury pie 50
spaghetti omelette 79
Muenster cheese 79
mussels, with pasta, pepper
& cheese 180–1

N

negroni cocktail 268–9

O

octopus
    'kebab' with potato & celery salad
        80–1
    with swordfish en papillote
        112–13
olive oil, extra virgin 12
olives
    in aubergine boats 84
    in bread salad 132–3
    Christmas fish 222
    Roman-style chicken 179
    with stewed rabbit & grapes 194
    stuffed, Ascoli-style 137
    stuffed conchiglioni 72–3
omelette, spaghetti 78–9
onions, red onion preserve 263
orange
    candied 60, 244
    sauce 230–1
ossobuco, with vignarola 156–7
oxtail stew, green 124

P

pancetta
    Ascoli-style stuffed olives 137
    in baked pasta 103
    pasta with carbonara sauce 106–7
    spaghetti omelette 79
    in vignarola 157
panzanella 132–3
Parmesan cheese
    artichoke parmigiana 109
    in cappelletti pasta cake 114
    rice & lemon sole timbable 184
    stuffed courgette flowers 138–9
    tea sandwiches (*tramezzini*) 146
parsnips, beetroot & apple salad 183
pasta 12
    with Amatriciana sauce 193
    baked, with asparagus, pancetta
        & provolone 102–3
    bucatini with clams & minty
        potatoes 154–5
    cannelloni, ricotta & saffron
        121–3
    cappelletti cake with cream, ham,
        liver & peas 114–15
    with cheese, pepper & mussels
        180–1
    chickpeas & beans with black
        truffles & lardo 158–9
    conchiglioni, stuffed 72–3
    fusilli with garlic, olive oil,
        endives, chillies, capers &

breadcrumbs 290–1
maccheroni with artichokes,
    courgettes & ricotta salata 192
penne gratin, Campolattaro-style
    171
ravioli with broccoli, anchovies,
    tomatoes & ricotta 168–9
spaghetti with carbonara sauce
    106–7
tomato sauce for 254–5
pastry
    filo, stars 213–15
    flaky, fans 20–1
    savoury short 50
    sweet 60, 238, 240
peaches, poached in syrup 216–17
peanuts 181
pears
    caramelized with *saltimbocca*
        287
    chocolate, amaretti & tutti frutti
        cake 233
    ice cream fruits 228–9
peas
    in capelletti pasta cake 114
    in savoury pie with artichokes
        & ham 50
    with squid, avocado & tomatoes
        172–3
    in vignarola 157
pecorino cheese
    in bread salad 132–3
    & broad bean mousse 104–5
    celery pesto 124
    with Easter bread 211
    marinated anchovies 147
    pasta with Amatriciana sauce 193
    pasta with carbonara sauce 106
    pasta, mussels & pepper 181
    spaghetti omelette 79
    tea sandwiches (*tramezzini*) 146
penne, gratin 171
peppers, Roman-style chicken 179
pesto
    celery 124
    courgette 262
pie
    with artichokes, peas & ham 50
    cappelletti pasta cake 114–15
    custard 238–9
    ricotta & chocolate 240
    wrapped vegetable 51–3
pineapple, in mimosa cake 204–6
pistachios 86, 142
pizza
    mini, with tomato sauce 54–5
    pizzette rosse 54–5
    tomato sauce for 254–5

polenta
    cake with pumpkin & apple 58–9
    sandwich with baked sausage
        & cheese 144–5
pomegranate 96
porchetta 188
pork
    Ariccia-style with 'dragged'
        cabbage 188–91
    Ascoli-style stuffed olives 137
    in chicken galantine 142
    chops with greased bread 182–3
    guanciale 192, 193
    meatballs 117
    rib sauce, with gnocchi 94–5
    ribollita soup 196
potatoes
    Christmas fish 222
    croquettes 134–6
    minty, with bucatini & clams
        154–5
    & orange savoury cake 164–7
    with rice-stuffed tomatoes 66–7
    ricotta gnocchi with prawns &
        pistachios 86–7
    sea bream with potato crust
        160–1
prawns, with ricotta gnocchi 86
preserves
    grape & pecan jam 265–6
    red onion preserve 263
pretzels, baked sweet wine 42–3
prosciutto
    in chicken galantine 142
    in filled beef rolls 98
    mousse with sandwich wheels 56
    in penne gratin 171
    see also ham
prosecco 184, 294–5
provolone cheese
    artichoke parmigiana 109
    in baked pasta 103
    in courgette boats 84
    in filled beef rolls 98
    & sausage polenta sandwich 145
    spaghetti omelette 79
prunes 117, 212
pumpkin, in polenta cake 58–9
puntarelle salad 120

R

rabbit, stewed 194–5
radicchio, in agretti tart 98–9
ravioli, with broccoli, anchovies,
    tomatoes & ricotta 168–9
ribollita soup 196–7
rice 12
    & lemon sole timbale with

prosecco gravy 184–5
rice pudding tartlets 36–7
Roman-style balls 134–6
stuffed tomatoes with potatoes
66–7
ricotta 13
in agretti tart 99
anchovy & tomato ravioli 168
& chocolate pie 240
& coconut balls 202–3
fried cheese & egg balls 278
gnocchi with prawns & pistachios
86–7
& saffron cannelloni 121–3
salata with maccheroni,
artichokes & courgettes 192
& sour cherry roll cake 246–7
stuffed courgette flowers 138–9
tea sandwiches (*tramezzini*) 146
wheat & candied fruit cake 60
rosetta loaf, with mortadella,
stracchino cheese & mostarda
68–70
runner beans 96–7

S
sage, fried 287
salad
bread 132–3
fennel, olive, orange
& pomegranate 219, 221
parsnip, beetroot & apple 183
potato & celery with octopus
80–1
puntarelle 120
spelt, with courgettes, chicken
& goats' cheese 44–5
salami 211
salmon fillet with broad bean
& pecorino mousse 104–5
salmon, smoked, tea sandwiches 146
salt cod, with chickpeas 88–9
saltimbocca, Roman-style 286–7
sambuca, Roman-style 270–1
samphire 98
sandwiches 56, 71, 146
sardines 46–7, 147
sausage
baked, with polenta sandwich 145
on bruschette 46–7
cotechino 218–21
with lentils, leeks & fennel 284–5
pork rib sauce with gnocchi 94
scamorza cheese 84, 109
scarola, sautéed 112–13
sea bass
carpaccio with peaches, kiwi
& rocket 75–7

with potato crust 160–1
sea bream 160–1
semifreddo, almond biscuit & sweet
wine 236–7
shallots, & prunes, glazed 117
shortbread biscuit trio 57
soffritto 13
sorbet, frothy lemon 294–5
soup
bread & tomato soup 288–9
Lazio-style ribollita 196–7
white 125
spaghetti
with clams & minty potatoes
154–5
omelette 78–9
pasta with carbonara sauce 106–7
spelt salad with courgettes, chicken
& goats' cheese 44–5
spinach & bread with veal 279–81
squid, with peas, avocado
& tomatoes 172–3
staple ingredients 12–13
stars, filo pastry 213–15
stew
beef, with artichoke parmigiana
108–9
green oxtail 124
rabbit 194–5
stock, making 12–13, 125, 184
straccetti al marsala 279–81
stracchino cheese 69
strawberry granita 276–7
sweet treats
Carnival sweet dough balls 223
ricotta & coconut balls 202–3
swordfish, en papillote with octopus
& lettuce 112–13

T
taleggio cheese 138–9
tarallucci al vino 42–3
tart, agretti 98–101
tartlets, rice pudding 36–7
tea sandwiches (*tramezzini*) 146
timbale, rice & lemon sole 184–5
tiramisù, lemon 241–3
toast, sweet Melba 34–5
tomatoes
in Amatriciana sauce 193
in aubergine boats 84
in bread salad 132–3
bread & tomato soup 288–9
on bruschette 46–7
in pork rib sauce 94–5
rice-stuffed, with potatoes 66–7
ricotta & saffron cannelloni 121–3
Roman-style chicken 179

sauce 13, 254–5, 278
with squid, peas & avocado 172–3
stuffed conchiglioni 72–3
sun-dried, anchovy & ricotta
ravioli 168
tozzetti biscuits 256–7
tramezzini 146
truffles 142, 158, 171
tuna
Christmas fish 222
cream, stuffed lemons 148–9
sauce with veal 118–19
stuffed conchiglioni 72–3

V
veal
brain *suppli* 134–6
in chicken galantine 142
with Marsala, spinach & bread
279–81
ossobuco with vignarola 156–7
saltimbocca with pear, sage
& braised lettuce 286–7
Savoy cabbage bundles 74
with tuna sauce 118–19
ventagli 20–1
vignarola, with *ossobuco* 156–7

W
water chestnuts 196
wheat berries & candied fruit cake
60–1
wine, cooking 12

Ringraziamenti

ACKNOWLEDGEMENTS

I've spent the most incredible year making this book, which gorgeously enriched my life. I'm absolutely thrilled and overwhelmed with joy to be surrounded by a remarkable group of people who have provided an unbreakable chain of support that is nothing short of spectacular. Therefore my thanks go first and foremost to the extraordinary Octopus Publishing Group for the contagious enthusiasm of making my Roman gastronomic adventures an attainable achievement since day one. Among them:

My commissioning editor, Eleanor Maxfield, for confidently hiring me as a first-time author and allowing me to write this book, thus including me in the fine presence of the company's great authors, who have entertained and influenced me for so many years before this book even came to life. It feels such a triumph for me to be on this list.

The fantastic Alex Stetter for editing my book and giving me the chance to own my voice throughout the pages and supporting my vision all along. Thank you for sharing this journey with me.

Art Director Juliette Norsworthy. It was a privilege to get through the graphic and creative process with you. Thank you for your dedication and commitment.

Natalie Bradley, for always making sure I'm on time.

Caroline Alberti, for making this book look beautiful.

Caroline Brown, Kevin Hawkins and the sublime Publicity and Sales departments for so bravely and intelligently showing me the way in this tremendous industry and being so eternally optimistic.

Everything I've shown through this book I got by picking up that phone, talking about my ideas and being given a chance by my brilliant agent Federica Leonardis at Rogers, Coleridge and White. That changed my life. You're largely responsible for this *opera prima*; this would not have happened without you. Thank you for fearlessly stepping into this adventure and trusting and supporting me by way of sheer enlightenment, and for not putting a restraining order on my emails, even when you're on holiday.

The photography maestro David Loftus, who worked so hard to keep me safe and make me laugh, without whose incredible professionalism, talent and humanity this book wouldn't be the treasure it is. These pictures were sinfully fun to make and I hope it shows. Thank you for flawlessly adapting your images to my words.

The sweet and hugely gifted food and prop stylists Emily Ezekiel and Linda Berlin, for all their hard work during the photoshoot days. Thank you for embodying my faith in timeless women, those with a capital W, who should never take the back seat.

The designers at Fendi, Red Valentino, Renato Balestra and Beulah, who let me rove their closets and look pretty in their dresses to beautifully convey that *Dolce Vita* style. Sorry if I broke a few heels on *sanpietrini* (cobblestones) in the process.

La Belle Assiette for letting me bring my #foodhappiness into people's homes.

All my friends who've tested my recipes, for being so receptive and wild and funny and, much to my astonishment, happy at the outcome – particularly Ginevra Boralevi, Rodolphe & Maggie Frerejean Taittinger, Matteo Basilé & Teresa Emanuele, Francesco Ruspoli & Angelica Visconti, Arnaud de Giovanni, Anne Helia Roure, Helene Bernowitz.

Ringraziamenti

ACKNOWLEDGEMENTS

Giovanna Rispoli for having so generously hosted me at your Capri retreat, and for the calm, cool, sun-breezed days during which to work without interruption.

Anna & Sergio Gelmi di Caporiacco, for taking such good care of me during my writing process and beyond, providing me with a peaceful cocoon in which to write, a kitchen in which to test my recipes and warm hospitality. I'm eternally grateful for your unparalleled sense of family and patience.

Artico, you rock my life. Thank you for keeping me on track, thank God for your stubbornness, thank God for everything about you: all I value in life, you've given me. You truly made me want to be the best woman I supposed I never knew I could be.

I wouldn't have written this book had I not understood love and its tremendous magnitude, and for that I thank my beloved and glorious great-grandmother Nonna Ia, who was the most beautiful and brave woman I've ever known, encompassing all qualities a human being should be provided with. Thank you for your undivided love and generosity, and for showing me by example what endearing power it is to share life with and for others.

My dear brother Giuseppe, thanks for continuing to push the boundaries of what's possible. You are my earthly guardian angel whose wisdom and guidance I have always looked up to.

Profound thanks to the incandescent Instagram community for all the tips and the constant support.

I am grateful for being allowed to use the wonderful locations at Antico Caffè Greco, Trattoria Settimio al Pellegrino, Bar del Fico, Bar Perù and the farmers' markets on Via della Croce and Piazza Campo dei Fiori.

Last but not least, thank you to the heroism and courage of the butcher, the shoemaker, the artisans, the market traders – they represent a world of unmatched excellence. Their portrayal not only shines a light on those artisanal jobs that are too often left out, but it shows Rome and their passion, their vulnerability, their humour and their extraordinary depth, which are far too exceptional to be ignored. #foodhappiness and Roman tradition need to be upheld.

Eleonora Galasso is a food writer, blogger, teacher and Instagram sensation. Her love of food began at an early age: she was forbidden from entering her great-grandmother's kitchen, but she was allowed to taste the pasta to make sure it was *al dente*. As is often the case in life, an obstacle turned a girl's curiosity into a hobby and a career. She went on to train at the Ateneo Italiano della Cucina in Rome before completing a Master's degree in gastronomy and food culture. For her first cookbook, Eleonora travelled the Lazio region extensively, accumulating recipes and stories from an eclectic cast of characters and bringing them to life with her unique creative touch.

Today Eleonora zigzags between Rome and Paris, working as a journalist and running cooking workshops, as well as collaborating with major international food brands and companies.